Canon EOS R50 V User Guide

Master Every Button, Video Feature, and Autofocus Mode with Step-by-Step Instructions for Beginners, Seniors, and Content Creators—Includes Photo & Vlogging Tips

Randy Osborn

Disclaimer:

This book is an independent publication and is not affiliated with, authorized by, sponsored by, or endorsed by Canon Inc. or any of its subsidiaries. Canon®, EOS®, and any related model names, logos, and branding are trademarks or registered trademarks of Canon Inc., which are used solely for descriptive and educational purposes.

All product names, logos, and brands mentioned in this book are the property of their respective owners. The information contained in this guide is based on publicly available resources, personal experience, research, and practical testing. It is intended for educational and informational purposes only and should not be considered official Canon documentation.

While every effort has been made to ensure the accuracy and usefulness of the content, the author and publisher make no warranties or representations regarding the completeness, reliability, or applicability of the techniques, settings, or

3

recommendations presented. The use of any camera gear or shooting method is solely at the reader's discretion and risk.

Always consult the official Canon user manual or authorized Canon support for up-to-date product specifications, firmware changes, and warranty-related concerns.

By reading this book, you acknowledge that the author and publisher shall not be held liable for any loss, damage, or injury resulting from the use or misuse of the information provided.

Table of Contents

Preface

Unlock the Full Power of Your Canon EOS R50 V — Without the Overwhelm

If you've just picked up the Canon EOS R50 V and you're feeling excited… but also a little lost, you're not alone. Whether you're a total beginner, a senior trying digital photography for the first time, or a vlogger looking for the perfect YouTube starter camera, this all-in-one Canon EOS R50 V user guide is for you.

Written in plain English with no tech jargon, this is not your typical camera manual. This is a simple camera guide for older users, beginners, and creators alike — packed with step-by-step camera manual tips to help you confidently shoot photos and videos you're proud to share.

What You'll Learn Inside This Easy Canon Camera Tutorial Book:

- How to Use Canon EOS R50 V: From unboxing to your first photo, we walk you through everything with crystal-clear instructions and real-life examples.

- Canon R50 Setup Guide: Learn how to quickly charge your camera, insert your memory card, and walk through the touchscreen setup with ease.

- How to Shoot Video with Canon: Discover how to master Canon R50 video settings for YouTube, TikTok, and Instagram reels — even if you've never filmed before.

- Canon R50 Autofocus Tutorial: Say goodbye to blurry shots. You'll master autofocus face tracking Canon features, including face and eye tracking Canon and subject lock, perfect for vlogging and portraits.

- Camera Guide for Seniors: Designed for clarity, larger text, and slow-paced instructions, this book is ideal for digital photography for older adults or tech-averse users.

- Photography Book for Travelers: Learn to compose stunning landscapes, street scenes, and food shots while on the go with Canon R50 for content creators.

- Canon R50 YouTube Setup: Build your vlogging camera setup for beginners with microphone tips, clean lighting hacks, and audio clarity fixes.

- Canon Touchscreen Q Menu Explained: We decode the touchscreen so you can change settings on the fly without digging through menus.

- Canon R50 Camera Explained in Plain English: From ISO to white balance, we break down every button, dial, and option without overwhelming you.

- Best Camera Settings for Beginners: Whether you're capturing pets, people, or products, you'll know what to use — and what to skip.

- Beginner Photography Tips + Manual Mode: Learn how to shoot like a pro with a guide that grows with you —

including when and how to learn manual mode with Canon EOS R50.

- Best Beginner Video Settings for Canon: Confused by 24fps vs 60fps or 4K vs HD? We simplify it for you — no filmmaking background required.

- Canon R50 Tutorial for Vloggers and Creators: Create content on the move with tips tailored to everyday life — from kitchen recipe videos to walking market tours.

- How to Transfer Photos from Canon R50 to Phone: Use Canon's Camera Connect App with ease to share your work in real time.

- Canon Mirrorless Camera Tutorial for 2025 and Beyond: Future-proof your skills with the best Canon mirrorless camera guide 2025 — written with today's tools and tomorrow's creators in mind.

Whether you're searching for an easy guide to shooting YouTube videos on Canon, a Canon camera guide for YouTubers, or just want to shoot great photos with Canon R50, this book delivers practical help from day one.

You don't need to be a tech wizard. You just need a guide that *speaks your language* and helps you actually enjoy your camera. This is that book.

Perfect for anyone looking for a Canon R50 V manual for beginners, a beginner camera manual for YouTube, or a Canon R50 photography book for everyday life, this hands-on guide will take you from curious to confident — no confusion, just creation.

Introduction

From Confusion to Confidence—Let's Make This Camera Yours

You're holding a powerful camera in your hands. The Canon EOS R50 is small, lightweight, and beginner-friendly, but don't let its size fool you—it's a serious tool capable of producing stunning photos and videos worthy of professionals. Yet if you're like most new users, chances are you've felt some hesitation. Maybe even a little overwhelmed. Don't worry. That's exactly where this guide comes in.

Who This Guide Is For

This book was written with real people in mind—not tech geeks or lifelong photographers, but those who want to use the Canon R50 for life's real moments. Whether you're:

- A senior picking up your first mirrorless camera to capture memories of grandchildren, hobbies, or travel

- A complete beginner who doesn't know where to start and wants simple, jargon-free instructions

- A vlogger hoping to share stories on YouTube, TikTok, or Reels

- A traveler documenting sights, culture, and the beauty of the world with minimal gear

- A content creator building your brand one video at a time

…you are exactly who this book is for. If you've ever thought, *"I wish someone would just walk me through this, step-by-step,"*— you've found the right guide.

You don't need a photography degree to take great shots or produce sharp, cinematic videos. You just need the right kind of help— practical, clear, and designed for someone with your goals, not a camera engineer's.

Why the Canon EOS R50 V Is a Game-Changer

Canon created the R50 with one clear mission: to remove the technical barriers that usually stand between you and your creativity.

This isn't just a camera—it's a tool for expression, designed for everyday people who want more than what a smartphone can offer, but don't want to spend months learning every menu option.

Here's why the R50 stands out:

- **Lightweight & portable**: Easy to carry anywhere, from travel adventures to backyard cookouts

- **Uncropped 4K video**: Film crystal-clear content for YouTube or TikTok without technical headaches

- **Dual Pixel Autofocus** with face and eye tracking: Keeps your subject in focus automatically, even while moving

- **Vertical video mode**: Perfect for creators who want to shoot for social platforms instantly

- **Intelligent Scene Recognition**: It figures out the best settings so you don't have to

And most importantly—it has the potential to grow with you. The R50 is powerful enough that once you learn the basics, you'll still be discovering new ways to use it six months from now.

How This Book Is Different

Most camera guides read like instruction manuals—because they *are* instruction manuals. They're written by people who assume you already understand things like aperture, ISO, and focus peaking. This book is the opposite.

This is a conversation, not a lecture.

No technical jargon. No robotic instructions. No assuming you already know what every dial or symbol means. Each chapter was written to meet you exactly where you are: curious, maybe a little confused, and eager to get results fast without the overwhelm.

Inside, you'll find:

- **Step-by-step walk-throughs** in plain language

- **Real-world examples** of how and when to use each feature

- **Everyday scenarios** that reflect your life—not a professional studio

- **Photos and video ideas** to get you creating from day one

- **A 10-day photo/video challenge** that boosts your skills quickly with just one new activity per day

Whether you're looking to take better family portraits, film cooking videos, snap your handmade crafts, or document a bucket list trip—this book is built around *you*.

What You Can Expect in Just 10 Days

Confidence doesn't come from knowing everything—it comes from using what you know consistently. And that's exactly what this book is going to help you do.

By the end of 10 days, you'll:

- Set up your camera the right way (without guessing)

- Understand the essential buttons and menus

- Master autofocus, lighting, and the modes that actually matter

- Record clean, focused video with ease

- Know how to store, edit, and share your work

- Feel comfortable enough to say, *"I've got this."*

You'll go from, *"I don't want to mess anything up,"* to *"I know exactly how to get the shot I want."*

Let's Begin.

You don't have to be "tech-savvy." You don't need to memorize dozens of camera terms. You just need a little guidance—and that's exactly what this guide will give you.

Let's take the Canon EOS R50 and turn it from a confusing gadget into your go-to creative partner.

Day by day, setting by setting, shot by shot—this journey starts now.

Chapter 1

Unboxing to First Click — Setup Without the Stress

You've just received your brand-new Canon EOS R50. The box is crisp, the lens is gleaming, and you're filled with the quiet excitement of possibility. But somewhere between slicing the tape open and holding the camera in your hands, a new feeling creeps in—*uncertainty*.

Where do I even start?

What if I break something?

Why are there so many things in the box?

Don't worry. This chapter is your guided hand. In the next few pages, we'll go from unboxing to your very first photo, all without stress, confusion, or the need to Google every step. You don't need to be "technical." You just need someone to walk you through the beginning, like a friend who's done this a dozen times. That's what this chapter is for.

What's in the Box (and What You Actually Need)

Inside your Canon EOS R50 package, you'll usually find:

- The Canon EOS R50 camera body

- The kit lens (typically 18-45mm f/4.5–6.3 IS STM)

- A Canon LP-E17 rechargeable battery pack

- A battery charger

- A neck strap

- A user manual or startup guide

- And sometimes a USB-C cable (depending on your region)

Now, take a deep breath—you do not need to understand or use everything right now.

Let's break it down into what you *do* need to get started:

- Camera body — obviously the core of the system.

- Kit lens — for now, this is the only lens you need.

- Battery + charger — power up before anything else.

- Memory card — not included in the box, but you'll need one to take and store photos or videos (more on that shortly).

- Neck strap — optional, but handy to avoid accidental drops.

Set the manual aside for now. You have this book.

Charge Up: Battery and Memory Card Setup

Before you power on the camera, let's take care of the essentials:

Charging the Battery

1. Unwrap the Canon LP-E17 battery.

2. Plug the battery charger into a wall outlet.

3. Insert the battery until it clicks into place.

4. A red light will show it's charging. When fully charged, the light will turn green.

Charging usually takes about 2 hours if the battery is fully drained.

Inserting the Battery & Memory Card

Once charged:

1. Turn the camera off.

2. Open the bottom compartment by sliding the latch.

3. Insert the battery—the label should face outward.

4. Next, insert the memory card into the slot beside the battery. The label faces the back of the camera.

5. Close the compartment until it clicks.

Important tip*: The R50 doesn't come with a memory card. You'll need to buy one separately. Here's how to choose one:*

Best Memory Cards for the Canon EOS R50

For smooth performance, especially if you plan to shoot 4K video or burst photos, get a UHS-I SD card with these specs:

- **Speed Class**: U3 or higher

- **Video Speed Class**: V30 or higher

- **Recommended Brands**: SanDisk Extreme, Lexar

  Professional, or Samsung Pro Plus

- **Minimum Size**: 64GB (128GB is ideal if you shoot lots of

  video)

Avoid cheap, no-name cards—they can corrupt files or fail when you need them most.

First-Time Setup: Powering On & Initial Settings

Now that your camera is powered and ready, it's time to turn it on for the very first time. Let's walk through it together.

Power It On

- Rotate the power switch on the top of the camera from *Off* to *On*. The screen will light up.

Choose Language

- Tap the screen to select your language (e.g., English).

- Confirm with the *Set* button or tap it on the touchscreen.

Set Date & Time

- Use the dials or touchscreen to choose your region, then input the current date and time.

- Tap *OK* or press *Set* to confirm.

Set Time Zone

- Select your local time zone for accurate time stamping of photos and videos.

That's it! You've now initialized your camera settings.

The Mode Dial — Which One Should You Use?

Let's keep it simple. Your Canon R50 has several shooting modes, each designed for different situations. But for now, turn the mode dial to the green "A+" icon—this is Scene Intelligent Auto Mode, the best place to begin.

Why?

Because the camera does all the thinking for you. It chooses the right settings, recognizes faces, adjusts focus, and even tweaks lighting. Perfect for your first photo.

If you're itching to experiment later, there's Creative Assist Mode, Aperture Priority (Av), and Manual (M)—but we'll get to those in future chapters.

Optional Accessories for Beginners (That Actually Help)

While the camera is perfectly usable out of the box, a few beginner-friendly accessories can make your experience smoother:

- **Tripod**: For steady videos, self-portraits, or long exposures.

- **External mic**: For better audio quality (especially for vloggers).

- **Screen protector**: To avoid scratches on your touchscreen.

- **Camera bag**: Protects your gear while traveling.

- **Spare battery**: Because one always runs out at the worst time.

Take Your First Photo — Right Now

Let's do it.

1. Turn the mode dial to A+ (Auto).

2. Press the shutter button halfway to focus. You'll hear a soft beep and see the focus lock.

3. Press it fully to take the shot.

4. Turn the rear dial to review your image on the screen.

Congratulations—you've just taken your first Canon EOS R50 photo.

It doesn't matter if it's of your desk, a coffee mug, or your pet's curious face. What matters is that you did it—from unboxing to capturing your first image.

Where We Go From Here

Now that the camera is physically ready and you've experienced your first click, the next step is getting comfortable with how everything works—from buttons and dials to menus and shortcuts. That's what Chapter 2 is all about.

Remember, every expert once started with a single photo. Don't rush. Don't worry about getting it "perfect." You've already taken the most important step: starting.

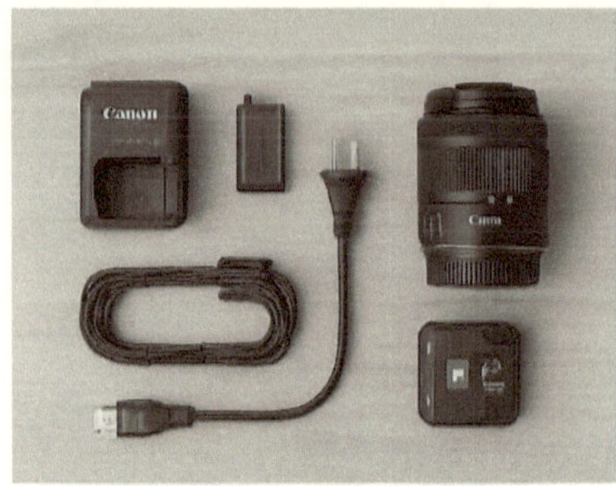

What's in the Box

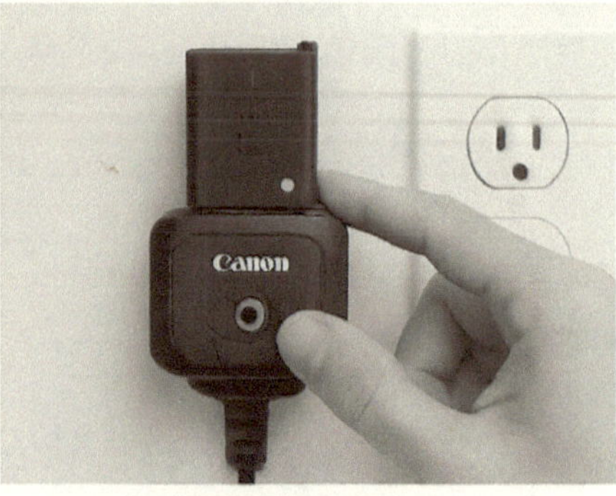

Charging the Battery

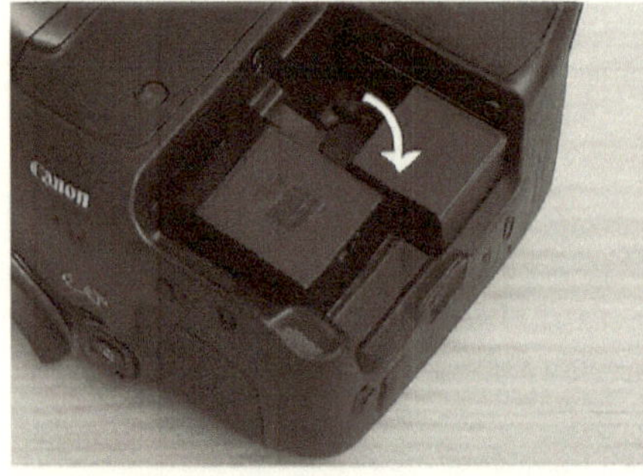

Inserting the Battery and SD

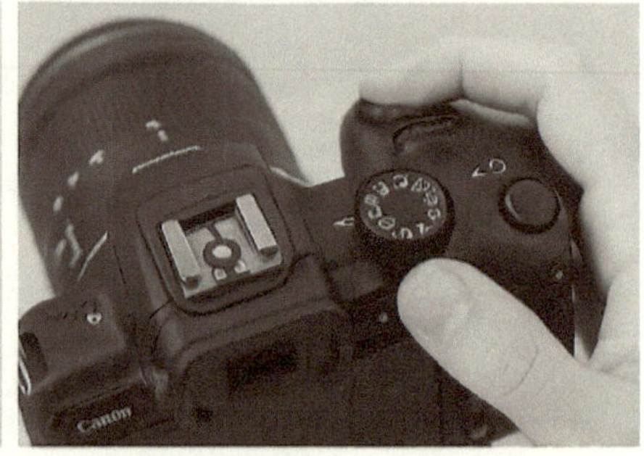

Mode Dial Set to Auto (A+)

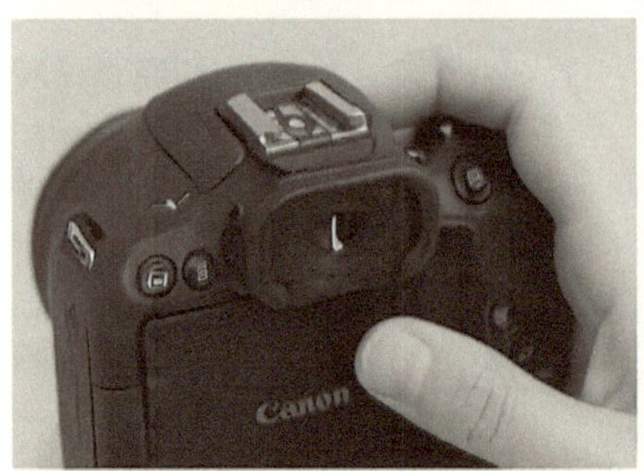

Taking Your First Photo

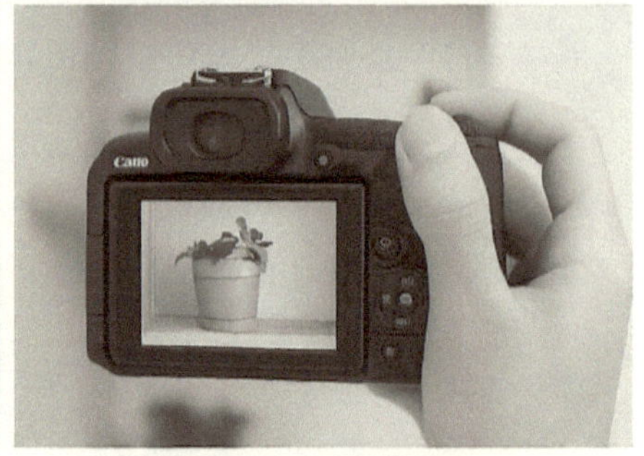

Taking Your First Photo

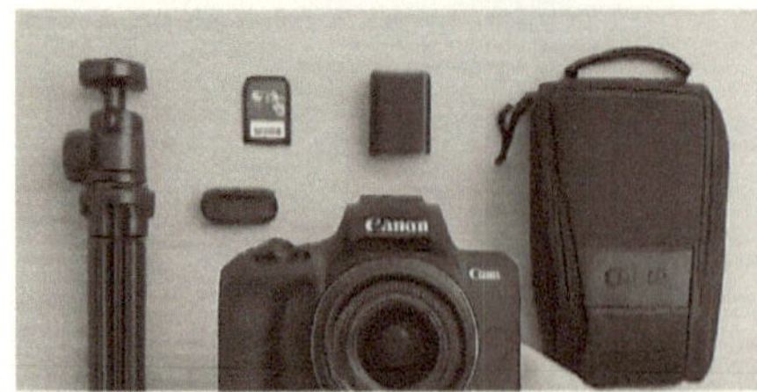

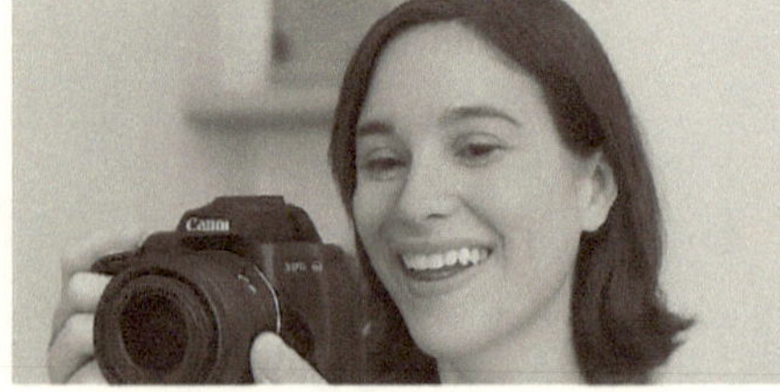

Chapter 2

Know Your Camera Like a Pro — Buttons, Dials & Menu Made Easy

So, you've charged the battery, inserted the memory card, and even snapped your first photo. But now you're staring at a camera body filled with mysterious buttons, switches, and icons you've never seen before. *Do I need to memorize all these? Will I ruin something if I press the wrong one?*

Relax. This chapter is going to demystify every button and dial on your Canon EOS R50—without drowning you in tech talk. You'll learn what everything does, which features to use now, which to save for later, and a few clever shortcuts that make handling this camera not just easy, but actually fun.

Let's Start at the Top — What's What

1. Power Switch (On/Off):

This tiny dial next to the mode dial is how you turn the camera on or off. Slide it gently—there's no need to force anything.

2. Mode Dial (The Big One):

This is the most important dial for beginners. It controls the shooting mode:

- **A+**: Scene Intelligent Auto (best for now)

- **CA**: Creative Assist (gives you simple control over blur, brightness, etc.)

- **P / Av / Tv / M**: Program, Aperture, Shutter, Manual (intermediate/advanced)

- **Movie Camera Icon**: Switches to video mode

- **SCN / Creative Filters**: Special effects and scene selections

We'll come back to these in later chapters, but for now, stick with A+ for photos and the movie icon for video.

3. Shutter Button:

Front-right, where your index finger naturally rests. Half-press to focus, full-press to take the photo. It's sensitive but responsive.

4. Main Dial (Behind the Shutter Button):

This scrolls through menu options or adjusts settings like aperture or shutter speed in certain modes.

What's on the Back — Your Main Control Panel

5. Touchscreen LCD (Fully Articulating):

This flips out, rotates, and folds in. It's also a touchscreen, just like your phone. Tap to focus, swipe through photos, and even access settings. You can navigate almost everything with touch alone.

6. Viewfinder:

Use this if you prefer looking through a lens instead of at the screen. Helpful in bright sunlight when the LCD is hard to see.

7. MENU Button:

Top-left on the back. Opens the full settings menu (organized in color-coded tabs). We'll only touch a few of these for now.

8. INFO Button:

Cycles through display styles. Want a cleaner screen or more data? Tap INFO. It won't break anything.

9. Q/SET Button (Center of Rear Dial):

This is the **Quick Menu**—a shortcut to your most-used settings like ISO, image quality, and white balance. You'll use this a *lot*. It's fast, intuitive, and easier than digging through the full menu.

10. Rear Control Dial (Circular Wheel):

Use this to navigate menus, scroll photos, or change settings in certain modes.

11. Playback Button (▶):

Lower-right. Tap it to view your photos and videos.

12. Trash Button (🗑):

Also in the lower-right corner. Use it to delete photos or clips you don't want. It will always ask "Are you sure?" before deleting—so no worries.

13. Record Button (Red Dot):

Located near the shutter button. Press this to start or stop recording video, even when the mode dial is set to video.

What Not to Touch (Yet)

As a beginner, some buttons or settings can lead to more confusion than clarity—at least for now. Avoid these until you're more comfortable:

- **Fn Buttons (Function Buttons):** These are customizable and may be blank or assigned to advanced features you don't need yet.

- **Manual Focus Switch on the Lens:** Leave this on AF (Auto Focus). Switching to MF will make it harder to get sharp images.
- **RAW Image Setting in Menu:** Stick with JPEG for now unless you plan to edit photos in software like Lightroom.

Hidden Gems You'll Love

Even as a beginner, there are three game-changing features that make shooting easier, faster, and more enjoyable:

1. Touchscreen Autofocus

Just tap the subject on the screen—your child's face, your pet, a flower—and the camera will lock focus instantly. This is especially useful for shooting off-center or filming video.

2. INFO Button Display Toggle

Tapping INFO cycles between simple and advanced displays. If the screen looks cluttered or too technical, tap INFO again—it's that simple.

3. Quick Menu (Q Button)

This is your secret weapon. Press it and you'll see an overlay with options like:

- Image quality

- Drive mode (single shot or burst)

- White balance

- AF method (face tracking, spot focus, etc.)

You can change settings *without leaving your current view*. That's powerful—and it's made for real-time decision-making.

A Visual Map of the Camera Body (Imagine

If you're holding the camera:

- **Top Right:** Shutter button, power switch, record button, mode dial

- **Back Top Left:** Menu button

- **Back Center:** Touchscreen, viewfinder, Q/Set, INFO, Rear Dial

- **Back Lower Right:** Playback and delete

- **Front:** Lens release button and grip

- **Left Side (behind door):** HDMI & mic input ports

- **Bottom:** Battery/memory card compartment

You don't need to memorize this. As you use the camera, your fingers will start to "learn" where everything is naturally. But it helps to know the layout now.

Real-Life Scenario: Switching from Photo to

Video Mode on the Go

Let's say you're in a café and you just took a photo of your coffee with a croissant. Now you want to record a quick clip of the steam rising from the cup. Here's how to do it—*smoothly and confidently*:

1. Rotate the mode dial from A+ to the movie camera icon.

2. Flip the screen toward you (or out sideways for a better angle).

3. Tap your subject on the screen to focus.

4. Press the record button (the red dot near the shutter).

5. Record your clip.

6. Press the red button again to stop.

7. Tap Playback to review it.

That's it. No menu-diving, no panic. You're now not just using your camera—you're creating content with it.

In Summary

You don't need to know *everything* about your Canon R50 to start taking incredible photos and videos—you just need to know what matters now.

This chapter showed you:

- What each major button and dial does

- Which features are beginner-friendly and which to ignore for now

- How to use the touchscreen, Q menu, and info button to simplify your workflow

- How to fluidly switch from shooting photos to capturing videos in real time

With this foundation, the R50 will stop feeling like an intimidating gadget and start feeling like a creative extension of your hand.

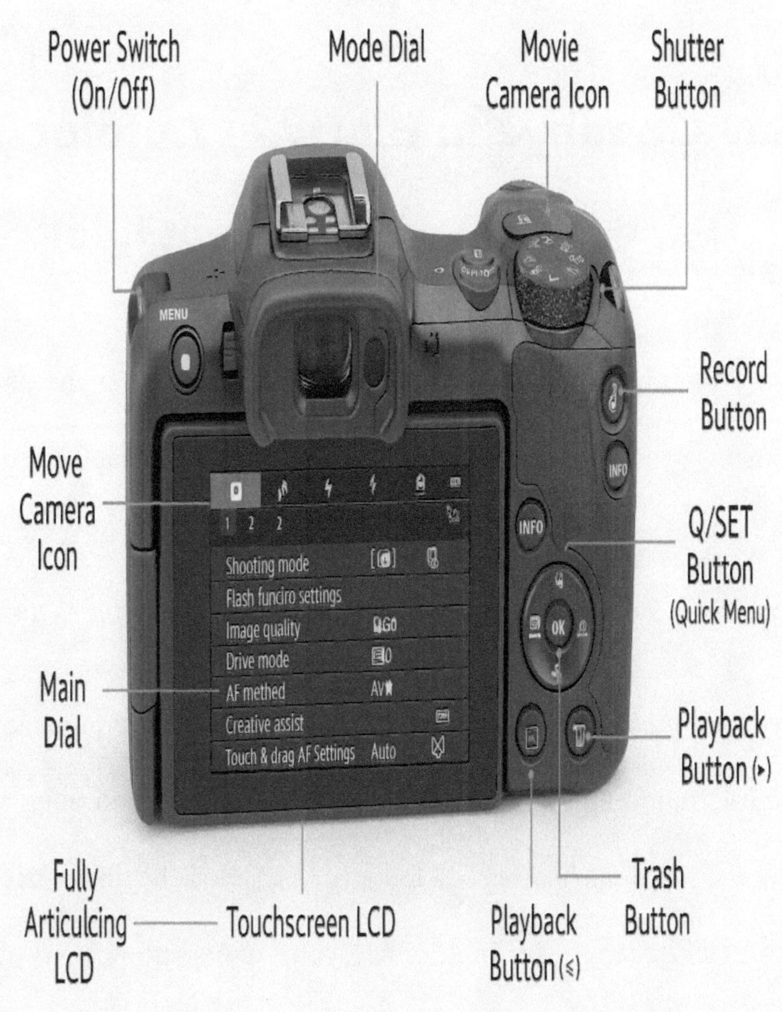

Power Switch (On/Off)
Mode Dial
Movie Camera Icon
Shutter Button
Record Button
Move Camera Icon
Q/SET Button (Quick Menu)
Main Dial
Playback Button (▸)
Fully Articulcing LCD
Touchscreen LCD
Playback Button (◂)
Trash Button
MENU
INFO
OK
Shooting mode
Flash funciro settings
Image quality
Drive mode
AF methed
Creative assist
Touch & drag AF Settings   Auto
1 2 2

Chapter 3

Say Goodbye to Blurry — Autofocus, Face Tracking & Subject Lock

Blurry photos are frustrating. You press the shutter at the perfect moment—your child is laughing, your dog is mid-leap, the sun is setting behind your partner's smile—and then… it's ruined. Out of focus. Soft. Fuzzy. That moment you wanted to preserve is gone.

If you've experienced this, you're not alone. In fact, it's the number one frustration among new camera users. But the good news? The Canon EOS R50 has one of the smartest, most beginner-friendly autofocus systems ever built. Once you understand how to use it, blurry photos can become a thing of the past.

This chapter will show you how to harness your camera's intelligent autofocus (AF), face/eye tracking, and subject detection to capture sharp, professional-looking shots—even in motion or on the go.

Why Photos Turn Out Blurry (and Why the R50 Can Fix That)

Blurriness usually happens for one of three reasons:

1. The camera focused on the wrong thing

2. The subject moved faster than the camera could adjust

3. You moved the camera during the shot

The Canon R50 combats all of these with Dual Pixel CMOS AF II, Canon's highly advanced autofocus system, which offers:

- 1,053 autofocus points covering nearly the entire frame

- Face and eye detection, even for pets

- Subject tracking, even while moving

- Auto refocusing during video recording

- And best of all — *you don't have to do any of the heavy lifting.*

Let's break down how to make it work for you.

Understanding Autofocus (AF) the Simple Way

Think of autofocus like your camera's eyesight. When you half-press the shutter, the camera looks around the frame and says:

"What does my user want me to focus on?"

Depending on your settings, it might guess correctly—or not.

The R50 gives you several autofocus modes, but here are the three that matter most right now:

1. Face+Tracking AF (for people, pets, and movement)

This is the go-to mode for:

- Portraits

- Children

- Pets

- Vlogging

- Any time you want the camera to prioritize a *person's face or eyes*

The camera identifies the subject's face (and eyes, if visible), locks focus, and tracks it—even if they move across the frame.

2. Spot AF (for still objects or products)

Best for static scenes:

- Food

- Landscapes

- Close-ups

- Flatlays or products

You manually select the point you want to focus on by tapping the screen.

3. Whole Area AF (for unpredictable motion)

Ideal for fast-moving scenes where there isn't a clear subject:

- Crowds

- Travel scenes

- Kids running around

- Pets playing

The camera analyzes the entire scene and tries to focus on what it deems most important. It's smart—but not perfect. That's why Face+Tracking is usually better when people or animals are involved.

Activating Face and Eye Tracking (For Humans & Pets)

Let's get to the good stuff: sharp portraits, vlog shots, and action photos. Here's how to set up face and eye tracking in your Canon R50:

Step-by-Step:

1. Turn your Mode Dial to *A+*, *Creative Assist*, or *Video* mode.

2. Press the Q (Quick Menu) button.

3. Scroll to AF Method (usually represented by a box with a
    face icon).

4. Choose Face+Tracking AF.

5. Make sure Eye Detection AF is set to *On*.

Now point the camera at someone's face—it should instantly show
a white box around it. When the eye becomes visible, it'll shift to a
smaller box over the eye.

That's your camera tracking and locking focus on the most
important part of the face.

For pets:

- If you're photographing a dog or cat, the R50 can usually
  recognize their face and eyes as well.

- Just enable Animal Detection AF in the full AF Menu
  (accessible via the Menu button → AF tab).

Tracking Subjects on the Move

Here's where the R50 really shines: tracking people or things in motion. Whether it's your toddler running through the yard, a friend dancing, or a fast-moving crowd while traveling, the camera can follow them with shocking precision.

How to use it:

- Set AF Method to Face+Tracking
- Press and hold the shutter halfway to engage focus tracking
- Keep the subject within frame—the camera will do the rest
- If subject moves too fast or exits the frame, it will try to reacquire focus

Pro tip: In video mode, the camera tracks without needing to hold the shutter—just point and record.

Refocusing While Recording Video

Many beginner creators struggle with blurry video or poor refocus performance when filming. Luckily, the Canon R50 makes it easy.

Here's what happens by default:

- The camera continuously evaluates the scene

- If something new enters the frame or moves, it tries to reassign focus intelligently

- You can tap the screen at any time during filming to shift focus to a new subject

Real-World Example:

You're filming your friend talking while walking, and a dog walks into frame behind them. The camera will keep tracking your friend's face unless:

- The dog becomes closer or more prominent, or

- You tap the dog on the screen, telling the camera, *"Focus here now."*

This touch-to-focus ability gives you full creative control, without the need for complicated menus.

Real-Life Scenario: Vlogging in a Busy Market

Let's say you're traveling through a colorful local market—bustling with people, moving carts, street food, and chatter. You want to vlog yourself talking while also capturing the world around you.

Here's how to do it:

1. Flip the LCD screen to face you.

2. Turn the mode dial to video.

3. Enable Face+Tracking AF with Eye Detection.

4. Tap your face on the screen once—it'll lock and track your movement.

5. Hit the record button and start walking and talking.

The camera will:

- Keep your face in focus as you move

- Smoothly shift focus if you pan toward something else

- Return to your face when you come back into frame

This kind of reliable autofocus in real-world motion used to require $2,000+ camera rigs and pro-level gear. With the R50, it's literally built in—and all it takes is a few taps.

In Summary

Blurry photos and videos don't have to be part of your story anymore.

In this chapter, you learned:

- Why autofocus is the key to sharp, consistent results

- The three best AF modes for beginners: Face+Tracking, Spot AF, and Whole Area

- How to enable face and eye tracking for humans and pets

- How to use touch-to-focus and subject tracking in real time

- How to film confidently in motion—vlogging, walking, capturing the chaos of life

With just these tools, you'll start producing shots that feel professional, polished, and alive with clarity.

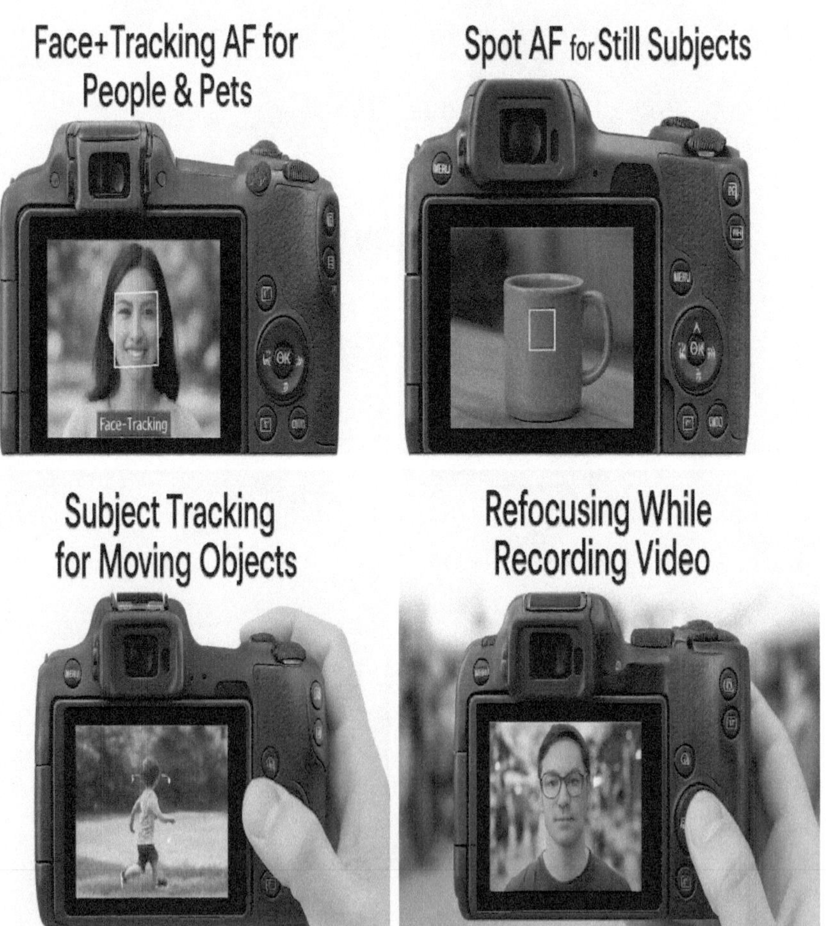

Chapter 4

From Boring to Brilliant — Camera Settings That Matter (and Which to Ignore)

You've probably seen amazing photos online—sharp, glowing, full of depth and life—and wondered, *How did they get it to look like that?* You point your Canon EOS R50 at the same subject and… it's just okay. Maybe flat. Maybe too dark. Maybe just... boring.

Here's the truth most people won't tell you: the difference between boring and brilliant is not expensive gear. It's knowing how to use the right camera settings at the right moment—and just as importantly, knowing which ones you can *ignore* for now.

This chapter is your shortcut to clarity. No confusing tech terms. Just practical help. By the end of this, you'll know how to:

- Use ISO, aperture, and shutter speed without getting overwhelmed

- Pick the best mode for everyday situations

- Make your photos look intentional, vibrant, and alive

  And you'll do it all with confidence.

Let's start by unraveling the settings that intimidate most beginners—and make them work for *you*.

The Three Settings That Shape Every Photo (Simplified)

At the core of every great photo are three settings photographers use to control how light enters the camera:

1. Aperture (the eye)

2. Shutter Speed (the blink)

3. ISO (the sensitivity)

You'll often hear these referred to as "the exposure triangle." Let's break each one down in the most beginner-friendly way possible.

Aperture = How Much Light Comes In (and How Blurry the Background Is)

- Think of aperture as the pupil of your camera's eye—it opens and closes to let in more or less light.

- A wide aperture (like f/2.8) = more light, blurry background (great for portraits).

- A narrow aperture (like f/11) = less light, everything in focus (great for landscapes).

Want that creamy background blur where your subject pops?

→ Choose a low f-number like f/2.8 or f/4.5.

Shutter Speed = How Long the Camera Sees

- Shutter speed is how long the shutter stays open when you take a picture.

- A fast shutter (like 1/1000) freezes motion (ideal for sports or kids).

- A slow shutter (like 1/10) creates motion blur or lets in more light (but may require a tripod).

Want to freeze your dog mid-jump?

→ Use a fast shutter speed like 1/500 or faster.

ISO = Light Sensitivity (But Watch the Grain)

- ISO tells your camera how sensitive to be to light.

- Low ISO (like 100) = cleaner image, less noise.

- High ISO (like 3200) = brighter image in low light, but adds grain.

Shooting indoors or at night?

→ Increase ISO, but try not to go over 3200 unless absolutely necessary.

But Wait… Do I Have to Change These Every

Time?

Nope. That's where your Canon R50's shooting modes come in.

These modes are your training wheels. They let the camera do the hard work *while you learn to steer.*

Beginner Modes That Make Life Easier

Let's go over the best shooting modes for real-life, everyday use:

A+ (Scene Intelligent Auto)

- *Best for:* Everyday snapshots when you don't want to think.
- The camera handles everything—focus, light, exposure.
- Great for first-time users, or quick moments.

CA (Creative Assist Mode)

- *Best for:* Beginners who want more control without technical confusion.

- Adjust background blur, brightness, color tone with simple sliders.

- You still shoot in Auto, but with *creative influence.*

Want to make your background blurrier? Slide the "background blur" bar and done.

This is a fantastic way to *learn visually* without knowing technical names.

Scene Modes Explained (Portrait, Landscape, Food, Sports, etc.)

Switch your Mode Dial to SCN, and you'll see a variety of scene-specific settings designed to optimize your photo with zero thinking.

Let's decode the most useful ones:

- **Portrait Mode:** Adds background blur, softens skin tones

- **Landscape Mode:** Sharpens details, boosts blues and greens

- **Food Mode:** Enhances color and contrast, especially in warm tones

- **Sports Mode:** Fast shutter speed to freeze movement

- **Night Portrait:** Slows shutter and adds flash to brighten low light portraits

- **Group Photo:** Widens focus area so everyone stays sharp

These modes tell the camera, *"Hey, I'm shooting a face,"* or *"This is a fast subject,"* and it adjusts accordingly.

Creative Filters: Fun, But Optional

The Canon R50 includes built-in creative filters—vintage, toy camera effect, soft focus, black and white, and more. They're fun for experimenting, but they *bake the look into your photo*, meaning you can't undo it later.

Use when:

- You want stylized shots without editing later

- You're feeling creative and want to experiment

Avoid when:

- You want to edit or retouch photos later

- You want to preserve natural color and clarity

When to Use Auto, Manual, or Creative

Let's keep this ultra-simple:

- **Use AUTO (A+)**

  When you're just starting out or don't want to miss a shot.

- **Use CA (Creative Assist)**

  When you want to control brightness, blur, or color *without learning full manual yet*.

- **Use MANUAL (M)**

  Only when you're ready to take full creative control and you understand ISO, aperture, and shutter speed.

Manual mode is powerful, but it's also like flying without autopilot.

Make sure you're comfortable before using it in important moments.

Real-Life Comparison: Portrait in Auto vs Manual

Let's walk through a real-world scenario:

Scene: Your friend is sitting by a window. You want to take a nice portrait.

Auto Mode (A+):

- Camera does everything.

- Background is *somewhat* blurry.

- Lighting is balanced, but not very dramatic.

- Safe shot, but may feel flat.

Manual Mode:

- You set f/2.8 (for strong background blur)

- Shutter speed: 1/200

- ISO: **400** (for indoor light)

- Result: A sharper subject, creamier background, natural light glowing across the face.

Takeaway: Auto gives you safety. Manual gives you mood, drama, and control.

But here's the truth—you can achieve 90% of that "manual magic" just by learning CA mode or Aperture Priority (Av). And that's what you'll start practicing in coming chapters.

In Summary

You don't need to master every setting to create brilliant images. You just need to understand:

- How light works (aperture, shutter, ISO)

- Which modes simplify the process

- When to use special scene options to suit your subject

- What to ignore (for now), so you can focus on shooting confidently

Your Canon R50 is not just a device—it's your creative partner. And now, it's no longer mysterious.

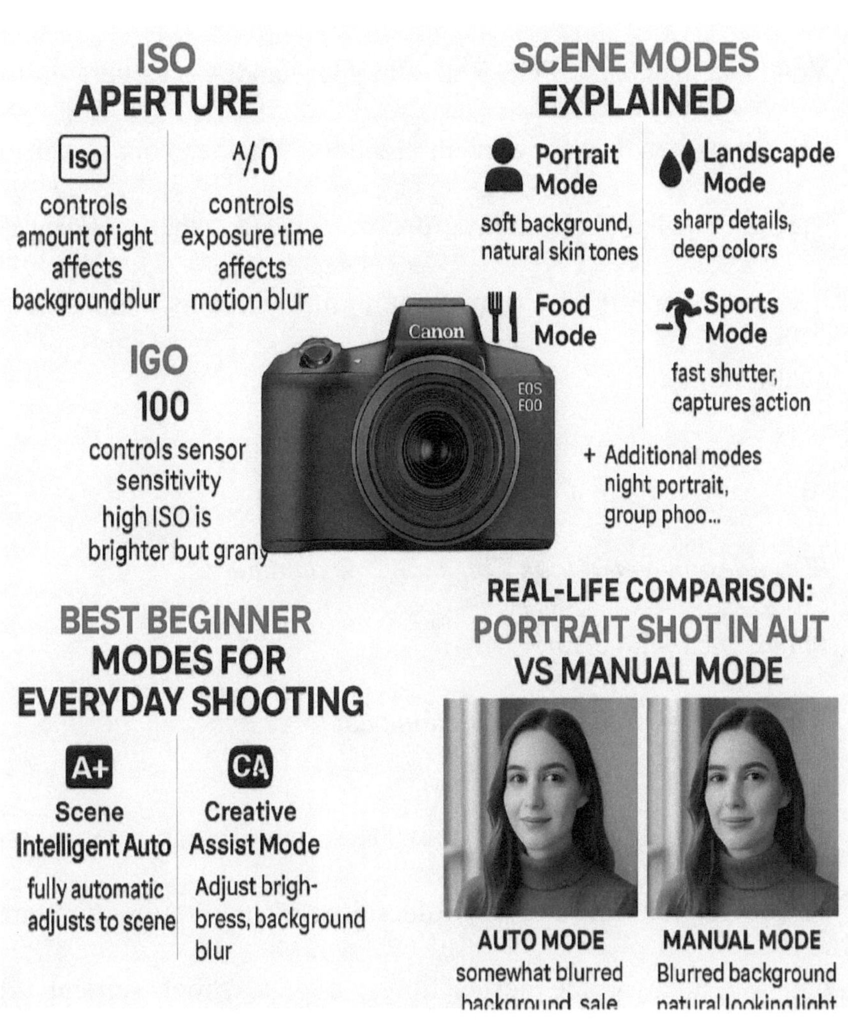

Chapter 5

Video Like a Vlogger — Mastering YouTube & Vertical Video

You have the Canon EOS R50 V in your hands—a camera built not just for photos, but for content creation. Whether your dream is to start a YouTube channel, grow on TikTok, share tutorials on Instagram, or simply film meaningful moments with beautiful quality, this camera was made for you.

And yet, there's that nagging feeling:

Why does my video look flat, shaky, or amateur?

Why is the audio echoey?

Why does it still feel like my phone could've done a better job?

This chapter is the turning point. Here, you'll learn how to make video that looks and sounds professional, even if you're just starting out. We'll cover the best settings, how to shoot vertical video effortlessly, what frame rates actually mean, and how to get crisp audio without complicated gear.

Let's unlock your Canon EOS R50 V's full video power—step by step.

Why the Canon EOS R50 V Is Built for Video Creators

The "V" in Canon EOS R50 V stands for video-first creators—and it's not just a label. Canon designed this camera with features tailored for you:

- Uncropped 4K video at 30fps
- Vertical video detection for social platforms
- Face and eye tracking that works flawlessly in motion
- Auto-leveling to keep your shot horizon straight
- Fully articulating touchscreen—perfect for self-filming
- Microphone input jack for cleaner audio

You don't need external recorders, gimbals, or studio lights to make high-quality content. You just need to know how to dial in the right settings—and that starts now.

Best Video Settings for YouTube, TikTok, and Instagram

Let's keep it platform-specific. Here's how to set up your Canon EOS R50 V depending on where you're posting your video.

For YouTube

- **Mode Dial:** Turn to the Movie Camera icon
- **Resolution:** 4K (3840×2160)
- **Frame Rate:** 24fps or 30fps
- **File Format:** MP4
- **AF Mode:** Face + Tracking
- **Eye Detection:** On
- **Picture Style:** Standard or Portrait
- **Stabilization:** Enable Movie Digital IS for handheld shots

Why 4K? YouTube compresses video, so starting with 4K preserves quality.

Why 24fps? It gives a more cinematic, natural look for sit-down videos, interviews, and storytelling.

For TikTok or Instagram Reels

- **Resolution:** 1080p or 4K (depends on your space/card speed)

- **Frame Rate:** 30fps or 60fps (smoother for handheld or action)

- **Orientation:** Shoot vertically (more on that next)

- **AF Mode:** Face + Tracking

- **Picture Style:** Standard or Neutral (to apply filters later)

- **Movie Digital IS:** On

Why 60fps? If you're moving, dancing, or doing tutorials, 60fps adds clarity and motion smoothness.

How to Shoot Vertical Video Automatically

This is where the Canon EOS R50 V stands out.

To shoot vertical video:

1. Rotate your camera 90° vertically

2. Open the Menu → Shooting Settings tab

3. Scroll to Auto Rotate Video → Set to On

4. Flip out the LCD so you can monitor your frame

5. Press Record

Your camera will now automatically flag the file as vertical, so it displays correctly on your phone, TikTok, or Instagram—no rotating in post-production required.

Tip: Use Portrait Scene Mode for a subtle beauty boost and background blur.

Frame Rate vs Resolution: What Do They

Mean (and What Should You Use?)

Let's break down the two terms that confuse most creators:

Resolution = Detail

- **1080p (Full HD):** Clear, smaller file size, faster upload

- **4K:** Higher detail, better for YouTube and editing, larger file size

Frame Rate (fps) = Smoothness

- **24fps:** Cinematic, great for storytelling

- **30fps:** Standard, everyday video

- **60fps:** Smooth, fast motion (sports, kids, dancing, movement)

- **120fps:** Super slow motion (in 1080p only)

Best combo for creators starting out:

→ 4K at 24fps for YouTube

→ 1080p at 60fps for Reels/TikToks

Audio Basics — Because Bad Sound Ruins Great Video

No matter how sharp your video looks, poor audio makes it feel cheap. That tinny, distant sound from your camera's internal mic can't compete with clean, close-up audio.

Here's how to fix that:

Use an External Microphone

The Canon EOS R50 V has a 3.5mm mic input—a huge advantage over many entry-level cameras.

Recommended beginner mics:

- Rode VideoMicro (compact, no battery)
- Deity V-Mic D4 Duo (captures both front & rear audio)
- BOYA BY-M1 Lavalier Mic (clip-on, ideal for talking videos)

Just plug the mic into the side port, attach it to your hot shoe (top of the camera), and start recording. The difference will be instantly noticeable—richer, clearer, more professional.

Lighting Tips for Video That Pops

You don't need expensive gear to get beautiful lighting. Here are three setups that work for almost everyone:

1. **Window Light:**

   - Film with the window to your side or front
   - Use white curtains to diffuse harsh sunlight
   - Add a reflector (or white foam board) opposite the window

2. **Ring Light or LED Panel:**

   - Great for even, front-facing lighting
   - Position slightly above and angled down for natural look
   - Avoid placing it directly behind the camera—it flattens the face

3. **Kitchen or Desk Lamp (Budget Setup):**

- Aim it at a white wall or ceiling for soft bounce lighting

- Warm bulbs give cozy tones; daylight bulbs are crisp and neutral

Real-World Scenario: Filming a Recipe Tutorial

Let's say you're filming a simple cooking video—making banana pancakes. You want to show your face, hands, ingredients, and get clean audio and lighting.

Here's how to do it with your Canon EOS R50 V:

- Mount the camera vertically on a tripod

- Flip out the screen to monitor yourself

- Set to Portrait Scene Mode or Manual Video

- Use 4K at 30fps

- Plug in a clip-on lav mic (like BOYA or Rode) and attach to your shirt

- Film near a window for soft light or use a ring light above the kitchen counter

- Use face tracking AF so your camera stays locked on your face even if you move

- Tap the screen to shift focus to ingredients as needed

Bonus Tip: Record B-roll separately—close-ups of chopping, pouring, and sizzling—and stitch it in later. Your content will instantly look like a pro production.

In Summary

The Canon EOS R50 V isn't just capable of recording video—it's designed to make you look and sound amazing.

You've learned:

- How to choose the best settings for YouTube, TikTok, and

  Reels

- The difference between 24fps and 60fps, and when to use

  each

- How to shoot vertical video that's ready to post instantly

- Which microphones give you clean, clear audio

- How to light your videos naturally or on a budget

- How to film step-by-step content like a recipe tutorial with

  zero stress

BEST VIDEO SETTINGS FOR YouTube, TikTok or Instagram

- Mode Dial: Movie (video camera icon)
- Resolution: 4K
- Frame Rate: 24fps or 60ps
- File Format: MP4
- AF Mode: Face • Tracking
- Picture Style: Standard
- Stabilization: Movie Digital IS

HOW TO SHOOT VERTICAL VIDEO AUTOMATICALLY

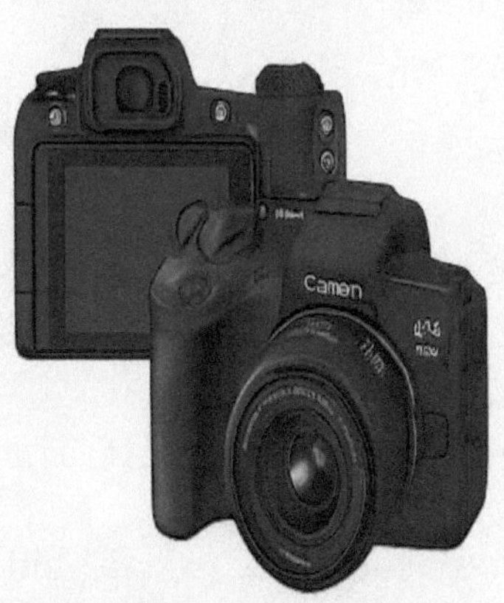

FRAME RATE (fps)

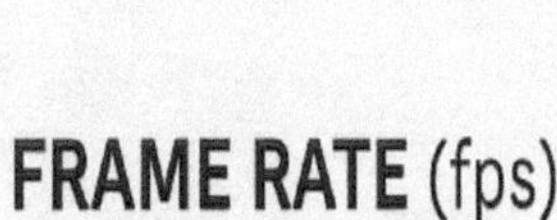

RESOLUTION

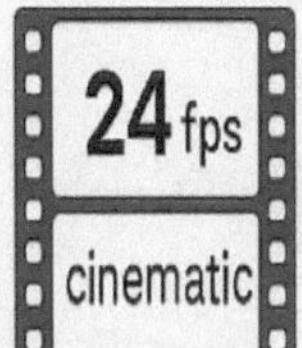

AUDIO BASICS
+ Which Microphone

AUDIO BASICS +
Which Microphone to Use

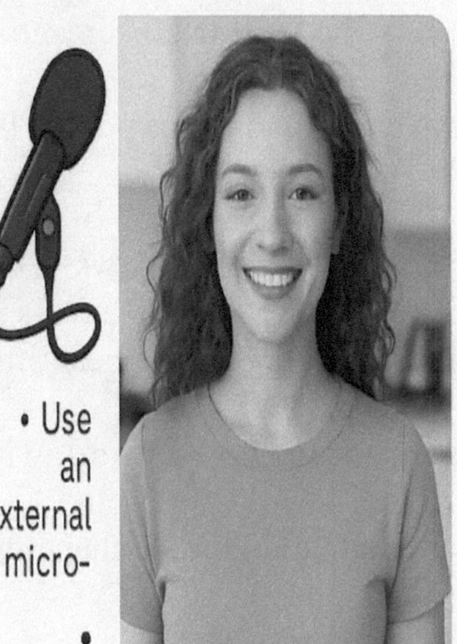

Chapter 6

Let There Be Light — How to Use Natural Light Like a Pro

So you've composed the shot. You've focused perfectly. But the photo still looks... off. Too yellow. Too dark. Washed out. Maybe your subject's face is hidden in shadow, or everything's bright except the thing you *actually* wanted to show.

Here's the hard truth: no setting, no lens, no editing software can save a photo that was poorly lit from the start.

But here's the great news: You don't need a studio, softboxes, or a full lighting rig to take beautifully lit photos or videos. You just need to understand how to work with natural light—the most accessible, flattering, and mood-enhancing light source in the world.

And the Canon EOS R50 V? It gives you every tool you need to control light without ever attaching a flash.

In this chapter, you'll learn how to find, shape, and master light—indoors, outdoors, and in every moment in between.

Best Lighting for Photos and Videos (Indoors vs Outdoors)

Let's start with the basics—what kind of light works best depending on your location.

Indoors

Best light source: A window

- Soft, directional light from a side-facing window gives depth and dimension to your subject.

- Use curtains or sheer blinds to diffuse harsh sunlight.

- Turn off overhead lights—they can create unflattering shadows or yellow tones.

Ideal times:

- Morning or late afternoon (not too harsh, not too dim)

Position your subject:

- Side-lit for portraits

- Front-lit for clean product or food shots

- Backlit for dramatic silhouettes

Outdoors

Best light source: The sky itself

- Overcast skies create soft, even light that flatters everything.

- Direct sun = harsh shadows and squinting. Seek shade, especially near walls or tree cover.

- Avoid midday when the sun is overhead and unflattering. Shoot during golden hour (more on this soon).

Pro tip: Use a white wall or building to bounce light onto your subject and reduce shadows.

How to Use Natural Light Without Reflectors or Flash

Many beginner photographers believe they need expensive gear to "control" natural light. Not true. All you need is awareness of light direction, distance, and diffusion.

Here's how to make the most of what's already around you:

1. Move Your Subject

- Step closer to a window.

- Turn them slightly until light hits one side of their face softly.

- If light is too harsh, shift them into partial shade or angle the camera differently.

2. Use Curtains as Diffusers

- Thin curtains create soft, creamy light.

- No curtains? Use a white sheet, baking paper, **or** frosted shower liner.

3. Use Walls, Boards, or Paper

- Place a white poster board opposite the light source to bounce light back onto the subject.
- Want drama? Use a black board to create shadows and contrast.

4. Avoid Direct Overhead Light

- Overhead lights cast nose and eye socket shadows. Turn them off.
- Stick with side or angled natural light for a cleaner look.

Golden Hour, Backlighting & Shadows — How to Work with Each

These light styles bring artistry and mood to your images—but only if used intentionally.

Golden Hour (Best Light Ever)

- Happens about 1 hour after sunrise and 1 hour before sunset

- Produces soft, golden, glowing light—flattering for skin tones and magical for scenery

- Faces light beautifully, and everything gets a warm tint

Best uses: Portraits, outdoor storytelling, romantic shots

Backlighting (Light Behind the Subject)

- Creates silhouettes or glowing edges

- Works well when the background is brighter than the subject

- Use exposure compensation to brighten the subject or embrace the silhouette

Best uses: Artistic portraits, moody product shots, nature

Shadows (And How to Use Them)

- Shadows add drama, texture, and story

- You can create interesting shapes using window blinds, leaves, or even furniture

- For high drama, use light from only one direction and a darker background

Best uses: Flatlays, moody food photography, lifestyle storytelling

How to Adjust Exposure in Real Time (Without Changing Modes)

Let's say your shot looks too dark or too bright. Do you need to jump into manual mode? Nope.

Use Exposure Compensation

This is your secret weapon.

On the Canon EOS R50 V:

1. Make sure you're in Auto, CA, or Av/Tv mode.

2. Press the Q (Quick Menu) button.

3. Look for the Exposure Compensation scale (it shows -3 to +3).

4. Use the rear dial or touchscreen to:

   o   Brighten the image: slide toward +1 or +2

   o   Darken the image: slide toward –1 or –2

5. Tap the shutter halfway to preview your change.

Pro tip: Use exposure comp *before* you shoot to get it right in-camera—less editing later.

Case Study: Taking Better Food Photos in Your Kitchen Window

Let's say you've just made a beautiful smoothie bowl or a stack of pancakes and you want to capture it. Here's how to light it like a pro, no flash, no fancy tools:

Setup:

- Find your brightest window, preferably one with soft indirect light (north or east-facing is best).

- Place your plate on a wooden table or neutral surface next to the window.

- Turn off all ceiling lights—they add yellow and confusing shadows.

- Use a white sheet of paper or foam board opposite the window to bounce light back.

- Use CA Mode and tap to focus on the center of the food.

- Adjust exposure using the Q Menu until it's just bright enough.

Want moodier vibes? Pull back the bounce light and let one side of the dish stay darker.

Want poppier colors? Shoot in the morning when light is cooler, or try Food Scene Mode on your R50 V.

In Summary

Light is everything—and it doesn't have to be complicated.

With the Canon EOS R50 V, you can:

- Harness window light for soft, studio-quality images

- Use golden hour and shadows for artistic depth

- Adjust exposure on the fly with simple tools

- Get professional lighting results using nothing but what's already around you

The difference between a photo that looks dull and one that *glows*? It's not your lens. It's not your camera. It's how you see and shape the light.

And now—you know how.

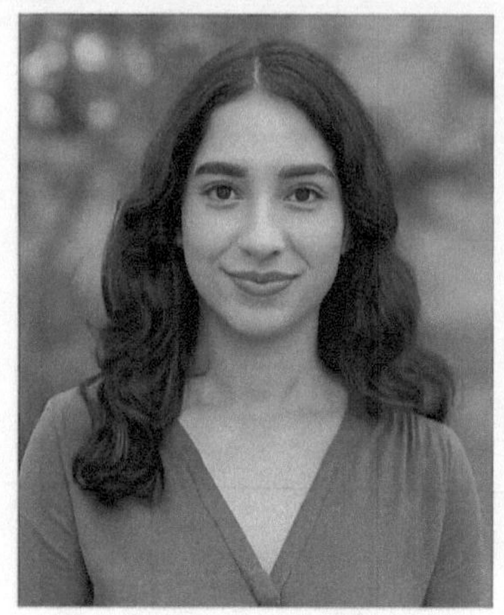

OUTDOOR
Overcast or shade
works best

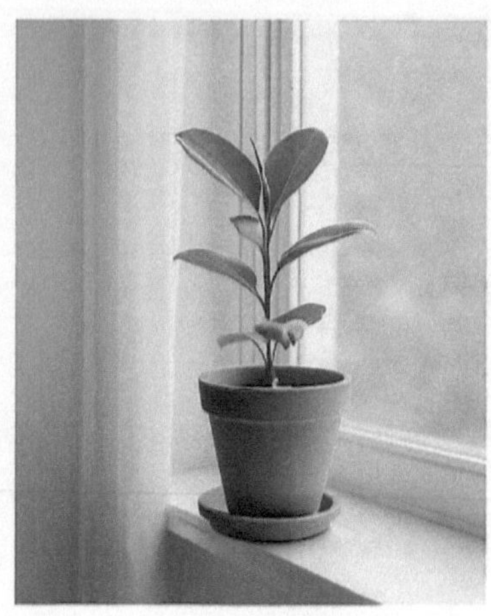

INDOOR
Use a window
for soft light

ADJUST EXPOSURE IN REAL TIME

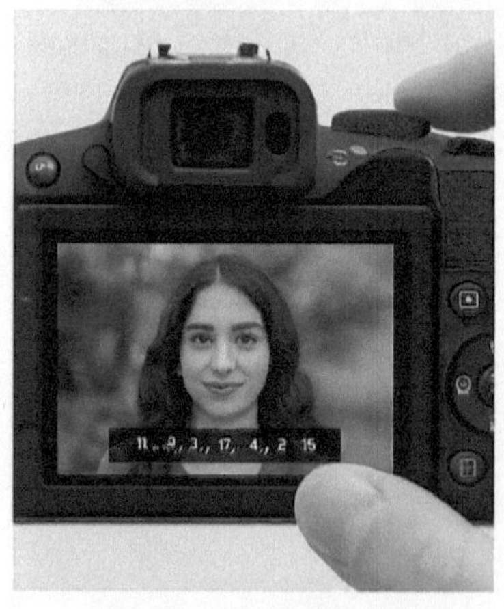

**FOOD PHOTOS
BY A WINDOW**
Turn off ceiling lights,

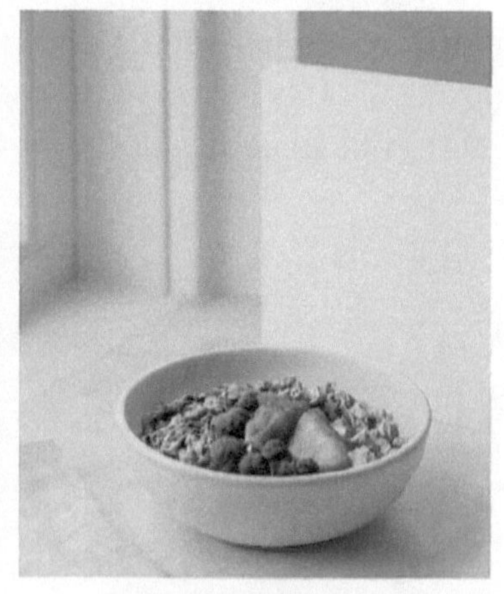

**FOOD PHOTOS
BY A WINDOW**
Turn off ceiling lights,

Chapter 7

Lens Know-How — What to Do With Your Kit Lens (and When to Upgrade)

You've been using the Canon EOS R50 V with the standard kit lens it came with—and maybe you've started to wonder:

Am I missing out by not having a better lens?

Do I really need to buy another one?

What's even the point of the lens I already have?

Before you go down the rabbit hole of lens shopping (and overspending), this chapter will help you:

- Understand exactly what your kit lens can and can't do

- Learn how to use it better for portraits, wide angles, and product shots

- Know when and why to upgrade—and what lens to get first

- And most importantly: how to change a lens safely so you don't damage your camera

Whether you're shooting YouTube videos, travel photos, food content, or family moments, the right lens helps you get the look you want—but you don't need a bag full of glass to get started.

What the Canon R50 V Kit Lens Can (and Can't) Do

If your Canon EOS R50 V came with the RF-S 18–45mm f/4.5–6.3 IS STM kit lens, here's what you're working with:

What It Can Do:

- **Zooms from wide to mid-range**: Great for landscapes, vlogs, and everyday scenes
- **Has image stabilization**: Helps reduce shakiness in video and handheld photos

- **Compact and lightweight**: Ideal for travel, street photography, and beginners

- **Fast and silent autofocus**: Perfect for video and face tracking

What It Can't Do:

- Doesn't create strong background blur (bokeh) for portraits

- Isn't great in low light (higher f-numbers mean less light enters the lens)

- Not ideal for tight indoor spaces or zoomed-in shots beyond 45mm

- Can produce a "flat" or "phone-like" look in certain creative situations

The kit lens is not bad—it's just basic. It gives you a wide view for vlogging and a bit of zoom flexibility. But when you're ready for more drama, clarity, or character in your shots, that's when you'll

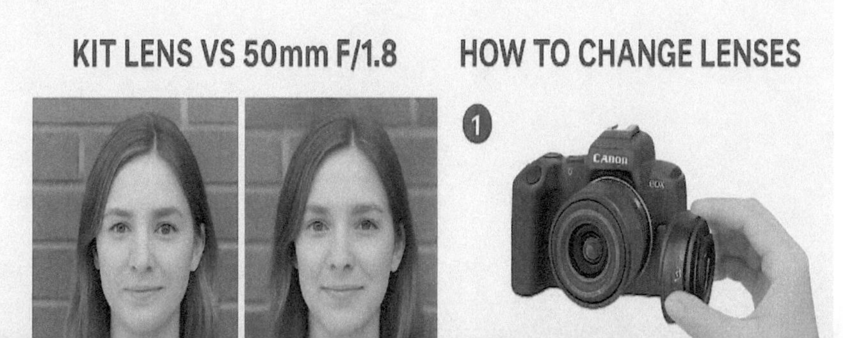

How to Use Your Kit Lens Like a Pro (Without Upgrading Yet)

Don't underestimate what you already have. You can stretch a ton of creative potential out of the RF-S 18–45mm by learning how to use focal length and composition intentionally.

For Portraits

- Zoom in to 45mm

- Stand a little farther from your subject

- Set the background a few feet behind them

- Use CA (Creative Assist) mode to increase background blur

This creates better subject separation, softens the background slightly, and minimizes distortion.

For Wide Shots (Landscapes, Interiors, Travel)

- Zoom out to 18mm

- Hold the camera steady or use a tripod

- Use the Landscape Scene Mode for rich detail and deeper depth of field

Avoid putting people too close to the lens at 18mm—it can exaggerate facial features and make them look cartoonish.

For Product Photos or Flat Lays

- Use the 35–45mm range

- Place your subject near a window (as covered in Chapter 6)

- Tap to focus manually for detail

- Slightly elevate or angle the camera to reduce distortion

You don't need macro mode. Just use good light and proper distance.

Beginner-Friendly Lenses for Portraits, Travel,

and Vlogging

When you're ready to go beyond your kit lens, here are the three best first upgrades, based on what kind of creator you are:

1. For Portraits & Background Blur

Canon RF 50mm f/1.8 STM

- Often called the "nifty fifty," it's small, affordable, and great for soft backgrounds
- f/1.8 aperture = stunning low-light performance
- Sharp focus on the subject, dreamy blur behind them
- Lightweight and under $150

Perfect for headshots, bokeh-rich food photos, and cinematic lifestyle content.

2. For Travel & Street Photography

Canon RF-S 18–150mm f/3.5–6.3 IS STM

- Versatile zoom: wide-angle to long-range

- Great for switching from scenery to close-ups without changing lenses

- Still compact, with built-in stabilization

- Ideal for people who want one do-it-all lens

3. For Vlogging & Ultra-Wide Video

Canon RF 16mm f/2.8 STM

- Ultra-wide, bright lens perfect for handheld vlogs

- f/2.8 aperture allows better lighting indoors

- Widens your background while keeping your face sharp

- Light, fast, and creator-friendly

Best for YouTubers, TikTokers, or anyone who self-shoots at arm's length.

How to Change Lenses Without Damaging

Your Sensor

Changing a lens may seem scary at first—what if dust gets in? What if I drop it? Don't worry. Follow this simple guide and you'll do it like a pro:

Step-by-Step:

1. **Turn off the camera.**

   This reduces static that attracts dust.

2. **Hold the camera face-down.**

   Gravity helps prevent dust from falling inside.

3. **Press the lens release button** on the right side of the lens mount.

4. **Twist the lens counterclockwise** (left) until it detaches.

5. **Quickly attach the new lens.**

   Match the **white or red alignment dots**, insert, and twist clockwise until it clicks.

6. **Do it in a clean, indoor space.**

Avoid changing lenses outdoors or in dusty environments if possible.

Extra Tips:

- Never touch the glass or the sensor inside.

- Keep rear lens caps on when lenses are stored.

- Use a blower (not canned air) to clean dust off the sensor gently if needed.

Example: Kit Lens vs Canon RF 50mm f/1.8

Let's compare the same portrait subject using both lenses, in the same lighting.

Lens Used	Aperture	Result
Kit Lens (45mm, f/6.3)	Narrow aperture	Image is clear but background

		remains in focus. Less depth.
50mm f/1.8 STM	Wide aperture	Subject stands out sharply. Background melts into a soft, creamy blur. Strong visual impact.

The difference is depth. With the 50mm prime, your subject pops. With the kit lens, the photo is nice—but flatter.

But remember: both are useful, depending on the look you're after. There's no "bad lens"—only the right tool for the shot you want.

In Summary

Your Canon EOS R50 V kit lens is a powerful tool when you understand how to use it—but eventually, your creative eye will crave more flexibility, blur, or reach. Now you know:

- How to use the 18–45mm range for portraits, wide shots, and products

- Which lens upgrades make sense (without spending thousands)

- How to change lenses safely and protect your sensor

- What kind of visual transformation to expect when you switch lenses

LET THERE BE LIGHT –
HOW TO USE NATURAL LIGHT LIKE A PRO

Best lighting for indoors vs outdoors

DARKER   DARKER

GOLDEN HOUR

DARKER   DARKER

Adjusting exposure in real tm

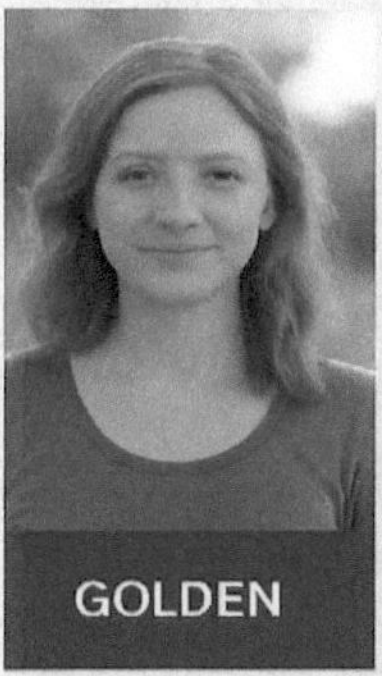

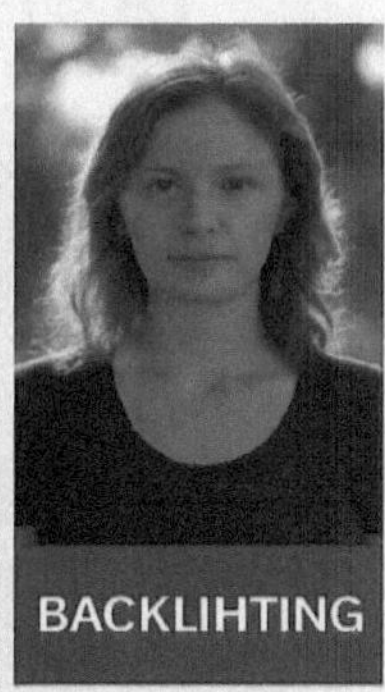

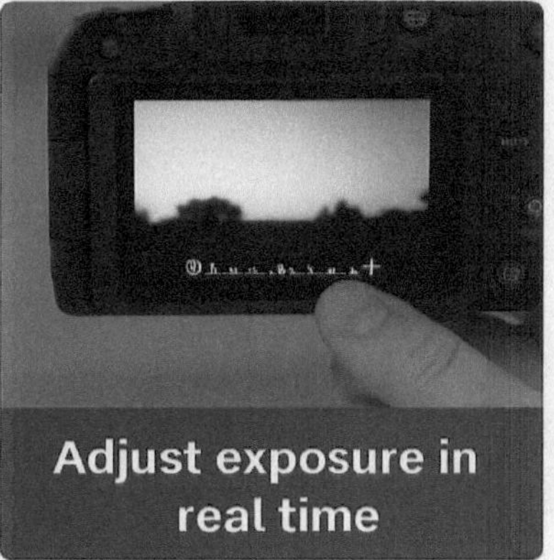

Case study: Taking better food photos near your kitchen window

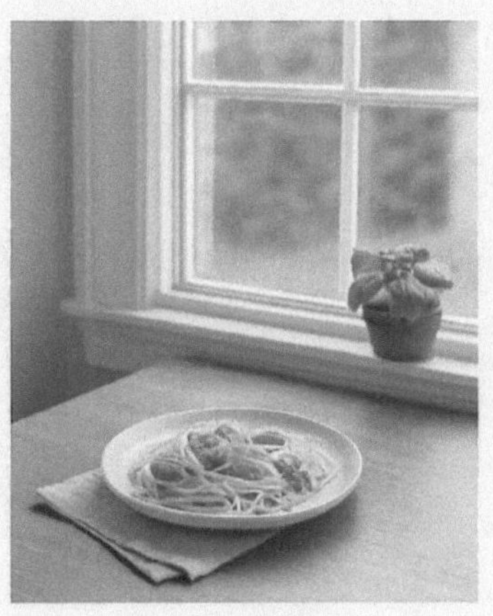

Chapter 8

From Snapshots to Stories — Composition, Framing & Creativity

You've got the camera. You've learned the settings. You've practiced lighting and even dabbled in manual mode. But something still feels off. Your photos are technically correct—well lit, in focus, properly exposed—but… they don't *feel* like anything.

You scroll through your gallery and think: *Why does this look boring?*

Why does someone else's photo of their coffee table look cinematic, while mine looks like a quick snap?

Here's the difference: composition.

The Canon EOS R50 V can capture incredible image quality—but composition is what transforms that image into a story. It's the art of what you choose to include in the frame, how you place it, and what emotional moment you're trying to share.

In this chapter, you'll learn how to:

- Use visual storytelling techniques like the rule of thirds, framing, and leading lines

- Shoot more compelling travel photos, selfies, and family portraits

- Apply these skills to everyday life: your dog, your food, your daily outfit

- Use your Canon EOS R50 V's built-in tools to train your creative eye

Why Composition Is More Important Than Equipment

Composition is what pulls someone into your photo. It's why some phone shots go viral while others taken with expensive cameras fall flat. It's not about *what* you're photographing—it's about how you're choosing to show it.

With a few simple techniques, you can go from snapping forgettable moments to crafting images that feel alive, deliberate, and share-worthy.

Let's start with three foundational tools that change everything.

The Rule of Thirds (and How to Break It Intentionally)

Imagine your photo divided into nine equal sections—three across, three down—like a tic-tac-toe grid. The rule of thirds says that placing your subject on one of the intersecting points will create a more dynamic, interesting image.

How to use it on the Canon EOS R50 V:

1. Go to Menu → Shooting Settings tab

2. Select Grid Display → choose the 3x3 grid

3. Use the grid lines to frame your shot—avoid putting the subject dead center

Portraits: Place the person's eye on one of the upper intersections

Landscapes: Align the horizon on the top or bottom third

Product shots: Let the item rest slightly off-center to give breathing space

Want to break the rule? Do it *intentionally.* Center your subject for symmetry, or break the grid when you want to draw attention in a bold way.

Framing: Turn the Ordinary into Art

Framing means using something within the scene to draw the viewer's eye toward your subject.

Examples:

- A doorway framing a person standing in a hallway
- Tree branches surrounding someone in a park

- Holding your coffee cup in front of a sunset

Framing creates depth, intimacy, and context.

On the Canon R50 V, you can tap to focus on your subject while allowing the frame (like leaves or windows) to stay soft in the foreground. This gives your image layers, even when you're in Auto or Creative Assist mode.

Leading Lines: Guide the Eye

Leading lines are visual cues that draw the viewer's gaze into the photo and toward your subject.

Look for:

- Roads

- Fences

- Staircases

- Shadows

- Table edges

When composing, ask yourself: Where does the eye go first—and where does it lead?

In travel photos, place a person at the end of a pathway or alley to create perspective. In flatlays, use utensils or flowers to guide attention toward your main item.

How to Shoot Travel Photos, Selfies & Family Portraits That Feel Alive

Great travel photos aren't just about showing what's *there*. They're about showing what you *felt* being there. The Canon EOS R50 V's articulating screen, face tracking AF, and vertical video support make it ideal for this kind of storytelling.

Travel

- Use wide focal lengths (18–24mm on your kit lens) to capture scenery
- Place people at one-third of the frame for drama

- Shoot at golden hour for soft, story-rich light

Selfies

- Flip out the screen

- Set to Video mode or Portrait scene mode

- Use face + eye tracking for perfect focus

- Tap to shift focus if you want to include a pet or prop

Add negative space (empty background) to emphasize mood.

Family Portraits

- Use Creative Assist mode to add background blur

- Frame the group loosely—tight crops feel cramped

- Use burst mode to capture natural expressions

- Tap on the person who's hardest to keep sharp (usually a toddler or pet!)

Real-Life Ideas: Make Everyday Life Look

Cinematic

Not everything has to be a trip or a special event. Some of the most beautiful shots come from ordinary moments framed with care.

Try these exercises with your Canon EOS R50 V:

Shoot Your Pet

- Get down to eye level

- Use Face + Tracking AF (yes, it works for dogs and cats!)

- Tap to focus and let the background fall away

Photograph Your Coffee Table

- Use the rule of thirds to place your mug or book

- Add soft side light from a window

- Place a hand or shadow to add storytelling

Capture Your Outfit

- Shoot in front of a clean wall with vertical video on

- Use a tripod or prop the camera up at waist height

- Tap focus on your face or chest

- Try black and white filter or neutral picture style for an editorial vibe

You'll start seeing beauty in the moments that used to pass you by.

How to Build Your Creative Eye Using the R50 V's Tools

The Canon EOS R50 V isn't just a camera—it's your teacher.

Here's how to use its built-in tools to train your eye:

- **Use the 3x3 Grid**: Practice rule of thirds until it becomes second nature

- **Review with Info Display**: After shooting, tap INFO to compare histograms, focus points, and framing

- **Try Creative Filters**: See how color grading affects emotion

- **Shoot in Black and White**: Forces you to focus on light, shape, and texture

Take one subject (like a chair or plant) and shoot it:

- From above

- From below

- In direct light

- Backlit

- Centered vs off-center

This type of repetition develops your vision. And when your eye improves, your photography transforms—without needing new gear.

In Summary

Your Canon EOS R50 V is more than capable of producing beautiful images—but it's your creative choices that make them meaningful. You've now learned:

- How to use rule of thirds, framing, and leading lines to tell visual stories

- How to elevate simple selfies, travel shots, and everyday moments

- How to build your creative instincts using the R50 V's settings and practice

Remember: your most powerful lens is your perspective.

FROM SNAPSHOTS TO STORIES

COMPOSITION, FRAMING & CREATIVITY

RULE OF THIRDS

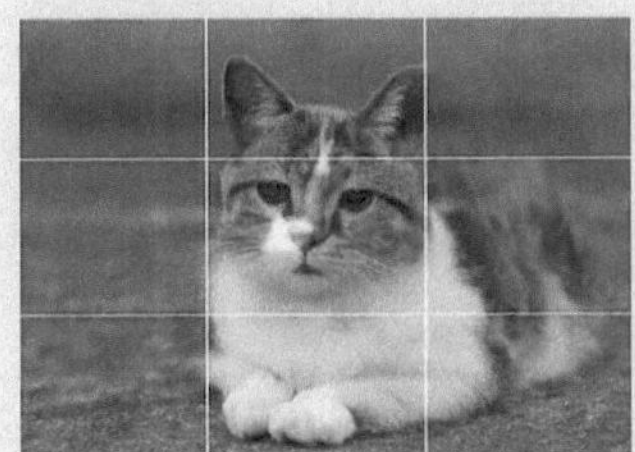

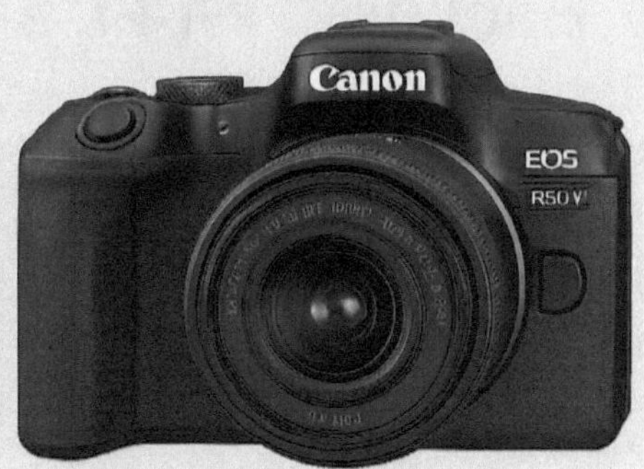

FRAMING

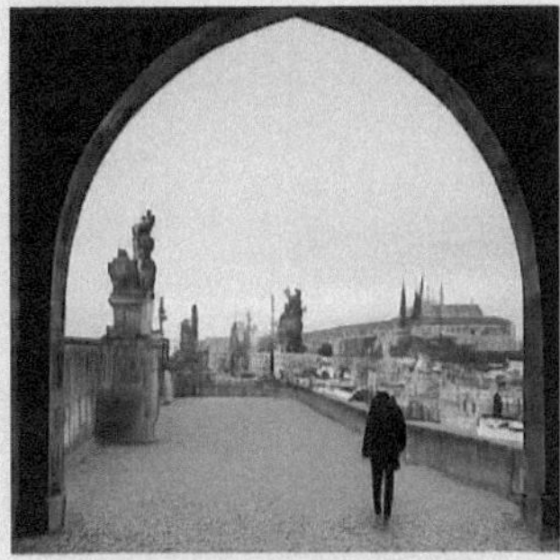

LEADING LINES

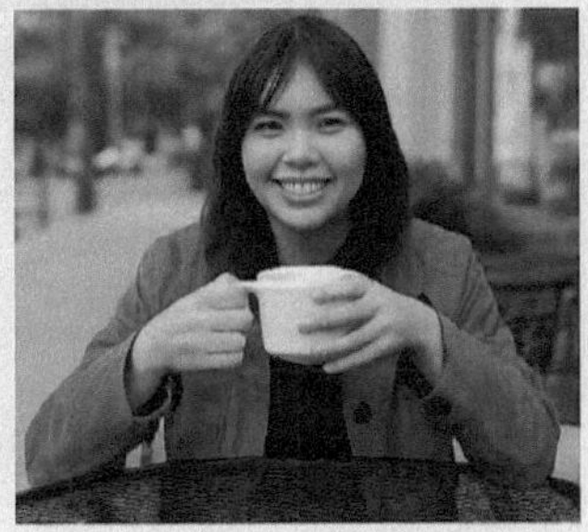

SHOT IDEAS:

- PET
- COFFEE TABLE OUTFIT

CREATIVE TOOLS

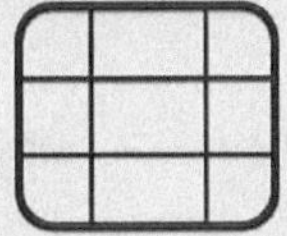

SHOT IDEAS

- PET
- COFFEE TABLE

Chapter 9

Store, Share, and Stay Safe —

Backups, Wi-Fi, and Maintenance

Problem Solved: "I don't know how to get photos off my camera or keep them safe."

So you've taken beautiful shots. You've filmed vlogs, travel memories, or a perfect coffee pour reel. But now what?

This is where many beginners freeze:

- *How do I send photos to my phone?*

- *How do I back everything up so I don't lose my work?*

- *How do I keep my Canon EOS R50 V running like new—without breaking it?*

This chapter gives you a real-world system for sharing, backing up, and maintaining your photos and videos, without needing to be tech-savvy. Whether you want to post to Instagram in under two minutes or store your footage safely for editing later, this chapter has you covered.

The Fastest Way to Get Photos to Your Phone: Canon Camera Connect App

The Canon Camera Connect app is your R50 V's best friend. It lets you wirelessly transfer images and videos straight to your smartphone for quick sharing.

How to Set It Up:

1. Download the Canon Camera Connect app on your phone (iOS or Android).

2. On the R50 V, go to Menu > Wireless Communication Settings > Wi-Fi/Bluetooth Connection.

3. Choose "Connect to Smartphone".

4. Select Easy Connection or use the QR code method.

5. On your phone, open the app, connect via Wi-Fi, and pair the devices.

Tip: You only need to do this once. After that, they'll auto-connect when nearby.

How to Use It:

- View and select photos directly from the camera on your phone screen.

- Tap and download your favorites instantly (without removing the SD card).

- Post to social apps in seconds, whether you're on a hike or in a café.

Transferring and Backing Up Like a Pro (Without Losing Files)

Even if you love posting from your phone, your full-quality files deserve a safer home—especially large videos and raw images.

Here's a three-tier system to make sure you never lose your work:

1. Manual Backup to PC (Safest for Video Creators)

How:

- Use the USB-C cable that came with your Canon EOS R50 V.

- Plug the camera into your computer and turn it on.

- The camera should appear like a USB drive.

- Drag and drop the files into organized folders by project or date.

If that doesn't work, use a card reader to transfer from the SD card directly.

2. Cloud Backup (For Instant Protection)

You can upload to services like:

- Google Drive

- iCloud

- Dropbox

- Amazon Photos (unlimited photo storage for Prime members)

Why this matters: if your computer or phone crashes, your memories are still safe in the cloud.

3. External Hard Drives (Long-Term Storage)

Invest in a 1TB or 2TB portable SSD or HDD. They're fast, reliable, and inexpensive.

Ideal for:

- Storing raw video files or large photo collections
- Archiving vlogs, client work, or passion projects

Always keep your external hard drive in a dry, padded pouch and away from heat.

Camera Care 101 — Maintenance Without

Fear

Your Canon EOS R50 V is built tough, but it still needs love. Here's how to care for it so it stays smooth and reliable for years.

Cleaning the Camera Body:

- Use a soft microfiber cloth (no paper towels!)

- Gently wipe the grip, back screen, and buttons

- Don't let dust build up around dials or ports

Cleaning the Lens:

- Use a lens blower to remove dust first

- Wipe in a gentle circular motion with a lens cloth

- If it's greasy or foggy, add a drop of lens cleaning solution

Never blow with your mouth or use your shirt. You could scratch the glass or fog the coating.

Cleaning the Sensor:

If you change lenses often, dust may land on the sensor. You'll notice faint spots in bright photos (like sky or walls).

If this happens:

- Go to Menu > Sensor Cleaning > Clean Now
- Don't touch the sensor manually unless you're experienced
- If needed, take it to a camera shop for a professional clean

Avoiding Memory Card Disasters & Battery Issues

A corrupted SD card or dead battery during recording can ruin an entire shoot. Here's how to prevent both:

Memory Cards

- Use Class 10 UHS-I SD cards from reliable brands (like SanDisk or Lexar)

- Avoid cheap, unbranded cards—they're prone to failure

- Format your card in the camera (not on computer) before a shoot

- Never remove the card while the camera is writing

Keep a second card in your camera bag. Always.

Batteries

- Use genuine Canon LP-E17 batteries for the R50 V

- Fully charge before long shoots or travel days

- Carry a spare to avoid missing moments

- Turn off auto image preview to save battery

- Don't leave the battery in the camera for weeks if unused

Real Scenario: From Snap to Instagram in Under 2 Minutes

Let's say you just took a beautiful photo of your coffee on your Canon EOS R50 V. Here's how to post it fast—without a laptop:

1. Turn on your R50 V

2. Launch Canon Camera Connect

3. Tap to transfer your photo

4. Open Instagram or Threads

5. Crop, caption, and post

All done before your coffee cools.

In Summary

Your creativity deserves protection. In this chapter, you've learned how to:

- Use the Canon Camera Connect app for instant phone sharing

- Back up safely to a computer, cloud, and external drive

- Clean your camera and care for your lens and sensor

- Avoid common issues with memory cards and batteries

- Share a photo to social media in under two minutes

Your Canon EOS R50 V isn't just a camera—it's a mobile studio. And now you know how to keep that studio clean, organized, and secure.

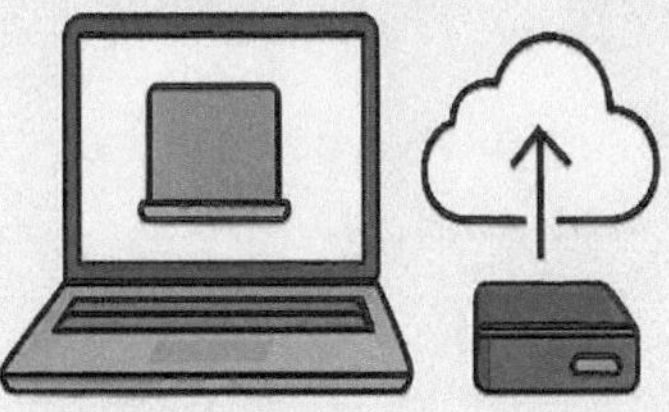

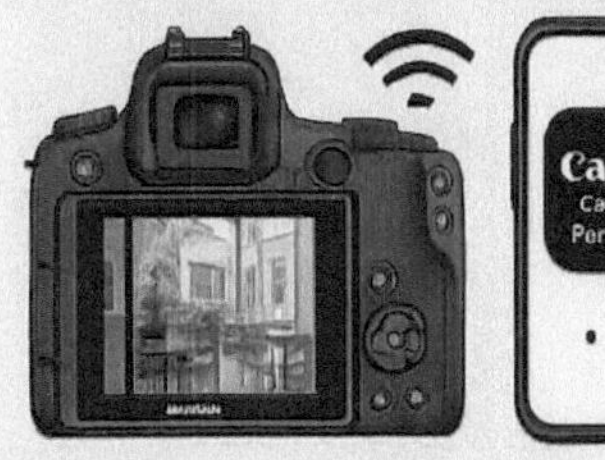

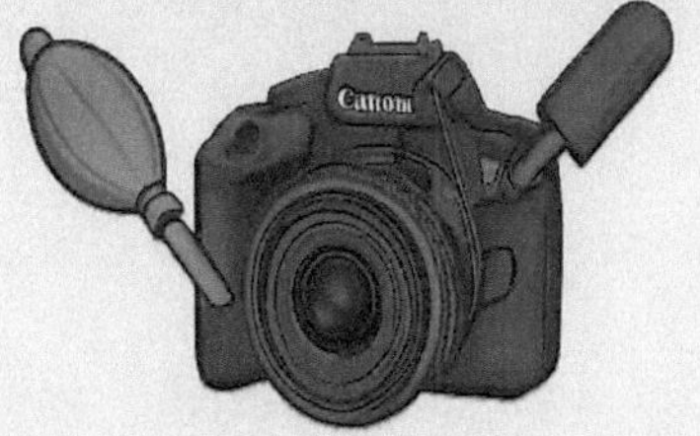

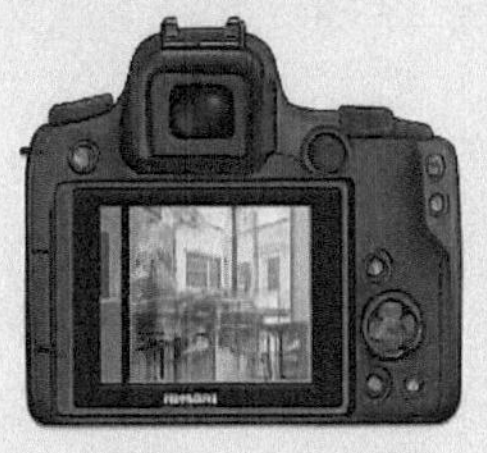
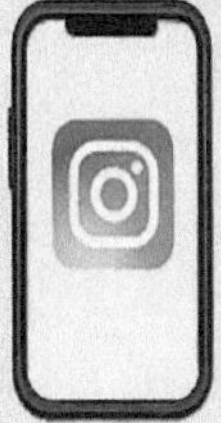

Chapter 10

10-Day Photo & Video Challenge — Build Confidence Daily

Problem Solved: "I don't know how to practice or improve."

You've set up your Canon EOS R50 V. You've learned to focus, shoot, record, and even share like a pro. But if you're still feeling like you don't *own* it—like it's not yet second nature—then what you need is practice.

Not practice in the abstract.

You need intentional, daily micro-missions that teach you a skill, build muscle memory, and—best of all—let you create something fun in the process.

This is your 10-Day Confidence Challenge. Ten days. Ten bite-sized tasks. Each one designed to help you:

- Understand a core camera feature

- Shoot in real-life scenarios

- See your progress in real time

And at the end? You'll have enough footage to create a one-minute highlight montage of your personal journey.

Let's get into it.

Your 10-Day Canon EOS R50 V Challenge

Each day includes:

- A creative mini-shoot

- A skill focus (based on earlier chapters)

- A real-life scene or subject you can capture anywhere

DAY 1: The Confident First Click

Mission: Take your first intentional photo in Auto mode.

Skill Focus: Camera grip, framing, shutter press.

Prompt: Shoot a favorite object in your room with good light.

DAY 2: Focus on the Eyes

Mission: Photograph someone (or your pet!) using face/eye detection autofocus.

Skill Focus: AF tracking, subject lock.

Prompt: Capture your subject blinking, smiling, or turning.

DAY 3: Shoot a 10-Second Vlog Clip

Mission: Film yourself talking using the selfie screen and movie mode.

Skill Focus: Frame rate, audio, lighting.

Prompt: Share what you're learning so far.

DAY 4: Create a Mood with Natural Light

Mission: Take two photos of the same object—once in harsh light, once in soft natural light.

Skill Focus: Light direction, shadows, exposure comp.

Prompt: Use your window, doorway, or balcony.

DAY 5: Composition Challenge — The Rule of Thirds

Mission: Frame a scene using the rule of thirds.

Skill Focus: Gridlines, off-center composition, leading lines.

Prompt: Photograph your meal, coffee table, or workspace.

DAY 6: Portrait Mode vs Manual Mode

Mission: Take a portrait of someone in Scene Mode > Portrait, then try to recreate the look using Manual Mode (Av).

Skill Focus: Aperture, background blur.

Prompt: Ask a friend or use a teddy bear as a model.

DAY 7: Product Photography at Home

Mission: Style and shoot a product like it's for Etsy or Instagram.

Skill Focus: Framing, zooming, lighting.

Prompt: Use a clean background (white cloth, wood, floor).

DAY 8: Movement + Autofocus

Mission: Capture a moving subject—person walking, pet playing, curtain blowing.

Skill Focus: Shutter speed, AI focus, tracking.

Prompt: Try both photo and video.

DAY 9: Vertical Reel Practice

Mission: Shoot a vertical video of your day in short clips (3–5 sec each).

Skill Focus: Orientation, transitions, shot variety.

Prompt: Walking outside, cooking, journaling—whatever feels true to you.

DAY 10: Your Best Shot Yet

Mission: Revisit your favorite challenge and try again—better.

Skill Focus: Apply everything you've learned.

Prompt: Reflect on what felt easy vs what still needs work.

Reflection Checklist

At the end of each day, ask yourself:

- What did I learn?

- What frustrated me?

- What would I do differently next time?

- Did I enjoy the process?

By Day 10, you'll see patterns, breakthroughs, and maybe even your creative style starting to take shape.

BONUS: Create a 1-Minute Video Montage of

Your Journey

Even if you're not an editor, you can use free tools like CapCut, InShot, or Canva video editor to stitch together your challenge highlights.

How:

1. Pick your 10 favorite clips or photos (1 per day).

2. Choose a short, royalty-free background track.

3. Add day labels or your reflections as text overlays.

4. Keep it under 1 minute for Instagram Reels or YouTube Shorts.

This isn't just a montage—it's a memory. It's your proof of progress.

In Summary

This isn't about perfection—it's about progression. And now you have a clear, creative path to:

- Practice every major function of the Canon EOS R50 V

- Build your camera confidence with daily tasks

- Develop a library of meaningful, well-composed, properly exposed photos and videos

- Celebrate your growth in a fun, shareable way

Remember: confidence doesn't come from knowing everything. It comes from doing something small, consistently, and watching yourself get better.

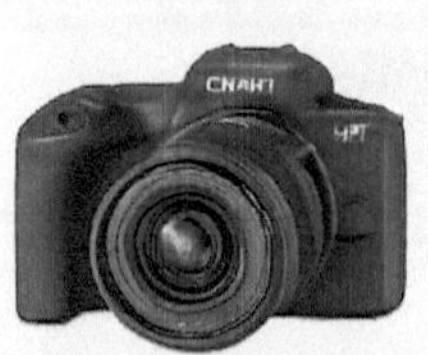

CANON EOS R50 V
10-DAY PHOTO & VIDEO CHALLENGE

 **THE CONFIDENT FIRST CLICK**

Mission: Take a photo in Auto mode

Prompt: *Shoat an object in your room*

 **FOCUS ON THE EYES**

Mission: Photograph a person or pet with face/eye detect AF

Prompt: *Capture a blink or smile*

 **COMPOSITION CHALLENGE – THE RULE OF THIRDS**

Mission: Use the grid lines to frame a photo

Prompt: *Shoot your meal or workspace*

 **PRODUCT PHOTOGRAPHY AT HOME**

Mission: Style and shoot an item

Prompt: *Find a clean background*

 **SHOOT A 10-SECOND VLOG CLIP**

Mission: Film yoursef talking in video mode

Prompt: *Share what you're learning so far*

CREATE A MOOD WITH NATURAL LIGHT

Mission: Take a photo in harsh and soft light

Prompt: *Use your window, doarway, or balcony*

 **PORTRAIT MODE VS MANUAL MODE**

Mission: Recreate a Portrait scene shot In Manual

Prompt: *Photograph a friend or stuffed aniinal*

 **VERTICAL REEL PRACTICE**

Mission: Record short clips of your day

Prompt: *Keep each shat 3–5 seconds*

BONUS

Create a 1-minute montage of your challenge

1. Select a clip or photo from each day
2. Add music + text labels
3. Export your video

Bonus Chapter

Troubleshooting Common Problems

Quick Fixes for Real People

Problem Solved: "My camera isn't working right, and I'm stuck."

No matter how beginner-friendly the Canon EOS R50 V is, there comes a moment when something goes wrong and panic sets in. Maybe the screen is black. Maybe nothing happens when you press the shutter. Maybe your Wi-Fi just won't cooperate—or worse, your entire video shoot ends up with no sound.

Before you toss the camera aside or think you "broke something," pause. Take a breath. Most problems with the R50 V are simple hiccups, not hardware failures. And this chapter is your calm, practical rescue plan for getting back to shooting in minutes.

Let's walk through the most common issues real people face—and how to fix them fast.

Issue #1: Camera Won't Turn On

What it feels like: You press the power button and… nothing. No light. No startup sound. Just a blank screen. It's tempting to think the camera is dead.

Quick Fixes:

- **Check the battery**: Remove it and reinsert. Make sure it's charged.

- **Try another battery** (if available): Sometimes new cameras ship with a low or faulty charge.

- **Ensure the battery door is fully closed**: The R50 V won't power on unless the door clicks completely shut.

- **Press and hold the power button for a full 2 seconds**: A quick tap may not be enough.

If the battery is charged and seated correctly, and it still won't power on, try plugging it into a wall outlet with the USB-C charger. If it powers on this way, the battery may be faulty.

Issue #2: Autofocus Not Locking or Blurry Shots

What it feels like: You point the camera at your subject, but the focus box keeps hunting—or never turns green. Your shots come out soft, or your subject is blurry.

Quick Fixes:

- **Ensure your lens is fully clicked into place.** A loose connection can affect autofocus.
- **Make sure you're not too close.** The kit lens can't focus properly at very short distances (especially under 0.25m).
- **Use the correct AF mode:**
    - For still subjects: use One Shot AF
    - For moving subjects: use Servo AF (AF-C)

- **Tap the screen to select the subject manually.**

- **Turn off Face/Eye Tracking** if it's confusing the scene (especially in group shots).

Extra Tip: Wipe the front of your lens with a microfiber cloth. A smudge can trick the camera into focusing incorrectly.

Issue #3: Wi-Fi Not Connecting

What it feels like: You open the Camera Connect app and wait… and wait… but your Canon EOS R50 V refuses to show up or link to your phone.

Quick Fixes:

- **Start fresh**: Delete the camera from your phone's Bluetooth/Wi-Fi settings and start the pairing process again through the Canon Camera Connect app, not your phone's system settings.

- **Ensure Bluetooth is turned ON on both devices.**

- **Hold the camera close to your phone during setup.**

- **Use the QR code method**: It's faster and more reliable than manual pairing.

- **Update your app**: An outdated version of Camera Connect can cause issues.

Reset Option (if all else fails):

Menu → Settings (wrench icon) → Wireless Communication Settings → Clear Settings

Then retry from scratch.

Issue #4: Images Are Too Bright (Overexposed) or Too Dark (Underexposed)

What it feels like: You take what you thought was a great shot, but the highlights are completely blown out—or everything is so dark you can't make out details.

Quick Fixes:

- **Use Exposure Compensation**:

In Auto or P mode, press the **Q button** and use the touchscreen slider to adjust brightness.

- **Tap your subject on the screen**: This tells the camera to expose based on that area.

- **Avoid shooting into direct sun** without adjusting settings.

- **Use Scene Modes**:

  - For bright snow or beach scenes → use "Bright" Scene Mode

  - For low-light indoor shots → use "Night Portrait" or switch to a lower f-stop and raise ISO

- **Check your ISO settings in Manual mode**: Too high = blown out. Too low = underexposed.

Pro tip: Use the histogram on screen when shooting to check if you're clipping highlights (spikes on the right) or crushing shadows (spikes on the left).

Issue #5: Video Is Too Shaky or Audio Is

Missing

What it feels like: You finally record your vlog or tutorial, but the footage is jittery and the sound is either terrible—or completely absent.

Quick Fixes for Shaky Video:

- Enable Digital IS:

  Menu → Shoot Settings → Movie Digital IS → Enable

- Use a tripod or handheld gimbal for walking shots.

- Hold the camera with two hands and tuck in your elbows when walking or moving.

Quick Fixes for Audio:

- Check if your external mic is plugged in all the way.

- Use the built-in mic in quiet environments only.

- Go to Menu → Sound Recording → Ensure "Auto" is enabled, or manually check input levels.

- Turn off wind filter indoors to avoid muffling.

Reminder: The Canon EOS R50 V does not have a headphone jack for monitoring. To test audio, record a short clip and play it back.

Issue #6: Memory Card Errors or Saving Failures

What it feels like: You press record or take a photo—and get an error about the card being unreadable, full, or too slow.

Quick Fixes:

- **Use a UHS-I U3 rated SD card (at least 64GB for video)** — especially for 4K.

- **Format the card in-camera** (not on your computer): Menu → Settings → Format Card

- **Don't remove the card while the red light is flashing** — this can corrupt files.

- **Avoid using old cards from other cameras or brands.** If needed, reformat before use.

Extra Safety Tip: Always carry a spare memory card and battery when traveling or filming important moments.

Final Words: The Confidence to Fix Anything

The Canon EOS R50 V was built with you in mind—yes, even when it hiccups. Learning how to solve problems on your own doesn't just make you more independent… it makes you more confident behind the lens.

Just remember:

- Take a moment to troubleshoot calmly.
- The answers are usually simpler than they seem.
- You now know what to do—and you've got the chapter to come back to.

And if all else fails? Power it off. Take out the battery. Breathe. Then start again.

You've got this.

COMMON TROUBLESCHING

CAMERA
WON'T TURN ON

- Check battery
- Try another battery
- Use correct AF mode
- Hold to focus
- Turn face Tracking

AUTOFOCUS
NOT LOCKING

- Check lens mounted
- Check focus distance
- Use correct AF moade
- Tap to focus
- Turn oft Face tracking

WI-FI
NOT CONNECTING

- Delete settings
- Check Bluetooth on
- Hold devices close
- Use QR code

OVEREXPOSED or
UNDEREXPOSED
IMAGES

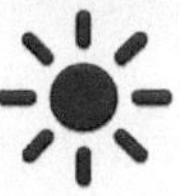

- Use exposure compensation
- Tap subject
- Avoid direct sun
- Use Scene moles

VIDEO TOO SHAKY
or AUDIO MISSING

- Enable IS
- Use tripod
- Check mic
- Set sound rectc auto

MEMORY CARD
ERRORS

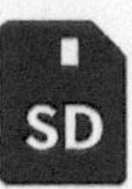

- Use UHS-I U3 card
- Format card in camera
- Avoid card in use
- Avoid old car

Conclusion

You're Not Just a Beginner Anymore

Celebrate Progress, Embrace Possibility

Take a second. Look back at the day you first opened the box and held the Canon EOS R50 V in your hands. Maybe it felt intimidating, mysterious—even a little overwhelming. Maybe you weren't sure what half the buttons did, or if you'd ever understand terms like aperture or 4K frame rate.

Now? You've come a long, long way.

You've taken your first steps, not just into photography or video, but into *visual storytelling*. You've learned how to navigate settings without fear, how to take sharper photos, how to film smoother videos, how to harness light, choose the right lens, and shoot with intention. You've moved from "accidental snapshots" to images that carry emotion, clarity, and voice.

This is more than mastering a camera. It's about unlocking a tool that helps you share how you see the world.

So pause and celebrate. You are no longer just a beginner.
You're a creator. A learner with momentum. A storyteller who now knows how to capture what matters.

Where to Go from Here

Now that you've built a foundation, here's how to take your growth further—without the pressure, and always on your own terms.

Try a Themed Project

- **30-Day Challenge:** Shoot one photo every day with a different theme: shadows, texture, hands, contrast, joy, motion, etc.

- **Vlog Mini-Series:** Pick a topic you love—food, fashion, your city, your pets—and create 3–5 short YouTube or TikTok videos around it.

- **Before/After Experiment:** Recreate one of your first R50 V photos using everything you've now learned. The difference will amaze you.

Level Up With Online Tutorials

Search for creator-specific tutorials based on your growing interests:

- "Canon R50 V bokeh tutorial"

- "Color grading Canon vlog footage"

- "How to shoot cinematic B-roll with kit lens"

- "Portrait lighting at home"

You'll find thousands of creators sharing niche tips on YouTube, Instagram Reels, and blogs. Pick one skill at a time and build on it.

Consider a Gear Upgrade (Optional)

You don't need to rush into new gear—but if you're feeling the creative itch, here are beginner-friendly upgrades worth considering:

- **A 50mm f/1.8 lens** for dreamy portraits and low-light photography.

- **A shotgun or wireless lav mic** for pro-quality audio in vlogs.

- **A ring light or LED panel** to improve indoor lighting.

- **A mini tripod with a fluid head** for more stable video panning.

Think of gear as tools, not trophies. Only invest when your creativity demands it—not just because someone on YouTube said you should.

Keep Improving Without Overwhelm

The biggest risk at this stage isn't getting stuck—it's burning out. The internet can flood you with advice, gear reviews, and pressure to be "better." But your growth doesn't have to be loud, fast, or public.

Here's how to improve gently, consistently:

- **Choose just one goal per week.** (E.g., "Learn manual focus," or "Film a coffee-making reel.")
- **Review your past work monthly.** See what you love. Note what you'd tweak. Let your own work guide your next steps.
- **Stay inspired.** Follow creators whose work feels human, not just polished. The ones who tell stories, not just chase trends.
- **Take breaks.** Sometimes stepping away gives you the fresh perspective you didn't know you needed.

Above all, remember: *progress is practice*. Every blurry photo teaches you. Every awkward shot means you showed up with intention.

Quick Reference: Canon EOS R50 V Setup Recap

When in doubt, here's your go-to checklist:

- Battery charged & inserted

- Formatted SD card (UHS-I U3 recommended)

- Mode Dial set to Auto or Video

- Q Menu: Face/Eye AF ON, Servo AF for motion

- Menu > Movie Digital IS: ON for video

- Scene Mode or Creative Filters for unique looks

- Frame rate: 24fps (cinematic) or 60fps (smooth)

- Wi-Fi + Canon Camera Connect synced

- Audio: Mic plugged in, levels on Auto or checked

- Exposure Compensation: Adjust for brightness

- Touchscreen tap-to-focus enabled

Screenshot this list. Tape it by your desk. It's your safety net.

10-Day Confidence Builder — Recap Planner

Here's your visual recap of the challenge you completed (or are about to):

Day	Skill Focus	What You Practiced
Day 1	First photo in Auto Mode	Basic camera setup + confidence click
Day 2	Face/Eye AF	Sharp selfies and portraits
Day 3	Switching to Video Mode	Smooth transitions + video button familiarity
Day 4	Lighting with Natural Light	Positioning, shadows, golden hour
Day 5	Manual Exposure (Optional)	ISO, shutter, aperture basics
Day 6	Kit Lens Zooming Practice	Wide angle vs portrait compression
Day 7	Composition (Rule of Thirds)	Framing objects, story-driven photos
Day 8	Creative Filter or Scene Mode	Stylizing images without editing
Day 9	Wi-Fi Sharing + Backup	Transfer images, cloud options
Day 10	Mini Video Montage	Music sync, edit basics, creative recap

Use this again anytime you feel rusty. Or restart with a new subject—pets, family, nature, fashion, food.

Final Words: You've Earned It

This isn't just a guidebook. It's your creative passport—one that helped you go from unsure to unstoppable. Your Canon EOS R50 V isn't just a camera. It's a mirror. It sees how *you* see the world.

So don't let the end of this guide be the end of your journey. Let it be the *beginning* of your confidence, your content, your story.

Your hands know where the buttons are now. Your mind understands the settings. And your heart? It's ready to shoot what matters most.

You're not just a beginner anymore.

You're a visual storyteller.

And the world is waiting to see what you'll share next.

Canon EOS R50 V
10-Day Confidence Builder

<table>
<tr><td colspan="2">QUICK REFERENCE</td></tr>
<tr><td>☐</td><td>Battery charged & inserted</td></tr>
<tr><td>☐</td><td>Formatted SD card (UHS-I U3 recommended)</td></tr>
<tr><td>☐</td><td>Mode Dial set to Auto or Video</td></tr>
<tr><td>☐</td><td>Q Menu: Face/Eye AF ON, Servo AF for motion</td></tr>
<tr><td>☐</td><td>Menu > Movie Digital IS: ON for video</td></tr>
<tr><td>☐</td><td>Scene Mode or Creative Filters for unique Looks</td></tr>
<tr><td>☐</td><td>Frame rate: 24fps (cinematic) or 60fps (smooth)</td></tr>
<tr><td>☐</td><td>Wi-Fi + Canon Camera Connect synced</td></tr>
<tr><td>☐</td><td>Audio: Mic plugged in, levels on Auto or checked</td></tr>
<tr><td>☐</td><td>Exposure Compensation: Adjust for brightness</td></tr>
</table>

RECAP PLANNER

Day	Skill Focus	What You Practiced
Day 1	First photo in Alito Mode	Basic camera setup + confidence click
Day 2	Face/Eye AF	Sharp selfies and portraits
Day 3	Switching to Video Mode	Smooth transitions + video button familiarity
	Lighting with	Positioning, shadows, golden hour

Acknowledgments

Creating this guide has been a journey made possible by more than just technical know-how—it's been powered by community, curiosity, and countless moments behind the lens.

First, to the everyday photographers—beginners, seniors, travelers, vloggers, and creators—who inspired this book: thank you. Your questions, frustrations, and breakthroughs shaped every chapter and reminded me why clarity matters.

To the online communities, forum contributors, and real-world Canon EOS R50 V users who openly shared their challenges and insights: your stories breathed realism into this work.

A special thanks to my editorial team, design collaborators, and research assistants for helping bring structure, precision, and visual support to every page.

Finally, to the readers picking up this book—whether you're just unboxing your Canon R50 V or finally ready to leave auto mode behind—thank you for trusting this guide as part of your journey. May it help you create images that not only look beautiful, but feel meaningful.

Keep shooting. Keep learning. The world is waiting through your lens.

About The Author

Randy Osborn is a trusted name in the world of camera education, known for transforming complex gear manuals into simple, step-by-step guides that anyone can understand. With over a decade of experience working hands-on with leading camera systems—from Sony and Canon to Nikon, Leica, and more—Randy has helped thousands of photographers, content creators, and everyday users get the most out of their cameras without the overwhelm.

Driven by a passion for accessible learning, Randy creates user-friendly books that strip away the jargon and focus on real-world usage. Whether you're shooting your first vlog, learning manual mode for the first time, or simply trying to take better family photos, Randy's guides are designed to make every setting click.

Each book combines clear instruction, practical tips, and

relatable language, making it easy for beginners and seasoned hobbyists alike to master their gear and capture life with confidence.

When he's not writing, Randy enjoys field testing new camera releases, hosting beginner-friendly workshops, and exploring hidden photography gems across the globe.

Join the journey to sharper skills and smarter shooting—one page at a time.